I0519184

Septuagint:

Esther

Septuagint, Volume 13

SCRIPTURAL RESEARCH INSTITUTE
Published by Digital Ink Productions, 2024

Copyright

Septuagint: Esther

Second edition. March 8, 2024

Copyright © 2024 Scriptural Research Institute.

ISBN: 978-1-998288-62-5

The Septuagint was translated into Greek at the Library of Alexandria between 250 and 132 BC.

The Septuagint was translated into Greek at the Library of Alexandria between 250 and 132 BC. Based on the reference in the postscript, the Vaticanus translation appears to have been translated in Jerusalem in 181 BC. Based on the dialect, the Alpha Text translation appears to have been translated in the Seleucid Empire earlier than 247 BC.

This English translation was created by the Scriptural Research Institute in 2019 and 2024, primarily from the Codex Vaticanus. Additionally, the Aleppo Codex and Leningrad Codex of the Masoretic text, and the Septuagint manuscripts 19, 93, 108, and 319 were used for comparative analysis.

The image used for the cover is an artistic reinterpretation of 'Esther Denouncing Haman to King Ahasuerus,' by Ernest Normand Long, painted in 1888. The original painting is currently on display in the Sunderland Museum & Winter Gardens, in Sunderland.

Table of Contents

TABLE OF CONTENTS

TABLE OF CONTENTS

Forward

In the mid 3rd century BC, King Ptolemy II Philadelphus of Egypt ordered a translation of the ancient Israelite scriptures for the Library of Alexandria, which resulted in the creation of the Septuagint. The original version, published circa 250 BC, only included the Torah, or in Greek terms, the Pentateuch. The Torah is the five books traditionally credited to Moses, circa 1500 BC: Cosmic Genesis, Exodus, Leviticus, Numbers, and Deuteronomy. According to Jewish tradition, the original Torah was lost when the Babylonians destroyed the Temple of Solomon and was later rewritten by Ezra the Scribe from memory during the Second Temple period.

It is generally accepted that there were several versions of the ancient Israelite scriptures before the translation of the Septuagint, mostly written in Phoenician and Aramaic, although the older sections of the Torah appear to have originated in Akkadian Cuneiform. There are two versions of the Book of Esther in the various copies of the Septuagint, however, neither originated at the Library of Alexandria. The common version of Esther is found in almost all copies, while the rare version is only found in four known manuscripts, numbered as 19, 93, 108, and 319. This edition includes both the Septuagint's versions, using the oldest surviving copies as source texts, the Codex Vaticanus, and Septuagint manuscript 319.

FORWARD

In addition to the two copies of the Book of Esther found in the Septuagint manuscripts, there are two additional surviving copies of the Book of Esther, one is found in the Masoretic Text, while the other is found among the Vetus Latina manuscripts. The Masoretic Text are the Hebrew translations of the ancient Israelite and Judahite books that form the core of the modern Tanakh which is used by Rabbinical Jews, while the Vetus Latina manuscripts are the Latin translations of the ancient books that were made before Jerome's official Latin translation of the Orthodox Christian Bible, published circa 405 AD. Each of these texts is unique, however, all appear to derive from earlier Aramaic texts.

The oldest surviving physical copy of Esther is found in the Codex Vaticanus, which dates to circa 350 AD. The version of Esther in the Codex Vaticanus is generally accepted as being the original version added to the Septuagint sometime in the 2nd century BC, however, it claims to have not been translated in Alexandria, like the rest of the Septuagint. The Vaticanus version of Esther includes the following postscript:

> In the fourth year of the reign of Ptolemy and Cleopatra, Dositheos, who he said was a priest and Levite, and Ptolemy his son, brought this letter of Purim, which they said was the same, and that Lysimachus the son of Ptolemy, that was in Jerusalem, had interpreted.

This verse was added to the end of the book and generally treated as part of the tenth chapter. It can be used to date the translation, but not easily due to the number of Egyptian kings and queens named Ptolemy and Cleopatra. If this was a reference to Cleopatra I Syra of the Seleucid Empire and her husband Ptolemy V of Egypt, it would likely be the year 181 BC, as Cleopatra I married Ptolemy V in 193 BC. If this is a reference to Cleopatra II and her husband Ptolemy VI Philometor, it would be the year 171 BC, as Cleopatra II co-ruled Egypt with Ptolemy V for the first decade of her first reign in Egypt.

After Ptolemy VI died in 145 BC, Cleopatra II married her younger brother Ptolemy VIII, however, their marriage does not appear to have lasted for four years, as he married her daughter Cleopatra III, sometime between 143 ad 139 BC. Cleopatra II was the sole ruler of Egypt during this era, until 127 BC, when she was driven out of Egypt by a coup led by Ptolemy VIII and Cleopatra III. This couldn't be a reference to Ptolemy VIII and Cleopatra III's fourth year, as they were reconciled with Cleopatra II after three years, and the three co-ruled Egypt. Ptolemy VIII and Cleopatra II died in 116 and 115 BC, leaving Cleopatra III, and her son Ptolemy IX Soter as co-rulers of Egypt. If this is a reference to Cleopatra III and Ptolemy IX, it would have been the year 112 BC. Cleopatra III then kicked Ptolemy IX out of Egypt in 107 BC, and replaced him as co-ruler with her younger son Ptolemy X, which means the year could be 103 BC. In 101 BC, Ptolemy X killed his mother and married one of his sisters.

The next couple this could be a reference to was Cleopatra V Auletes and her husband Ptolemy XII Tryphaena, which would make the year referenced in the postscript 75 BC. Their daughter Cleopatra VII Philopator later ruled between 52 and 30 BC, and was co-ruler with four successive men named Ptolemy: her father Ptolemy XII Auletes (52 to 51 BC), Ptolemy XIII Theos Philopator (51 to 47 BC), Ptolemy XIV Philopator (47 to 44 BC), and Ptolemy XV Caesarion (44 to 30 BC). Cleopatra VII did not co-rule with her father Ptolemy XII, or her husbands Ptolemy XIV and Ptolemy XIII long enough for any of these men to be the Ptolemy mentioned, however, her son Ptolemy XIII could have been the Ptolemy in question, making the year 40 BC another possible date the postscript is referring to. This means that the possible year that the book was translated in Jerusalem, are 181 BC, 112 BC, 103 BC, 75 BC, and 40 BC.

Nevertheless, the postscript specifically mentions the translation being made in Jerusalem, which therefore implies that Judea was under the rule of the Ptolemy and Cleopatra in question, or else there was no reason to have referenced them. The Greeks in Egypt were already using the Egyptian Civil calendar, with Greek names substituted for Egyptian, and that calendar would have been referenced if a Greek scholar in Egypt had added the note. In the Seleucid Empire, a modified version of the Macedonian calendar was in use, however, this is also not mentioned in the Vaticanus version. The only one of the couples named Ptolemy and Cleopatra who did rule Judea was Cleopatra I Syra of the Seleucid Empire and her husband Ptolemy V of Egypt, meaning the Vaticanus version of Esther was most likely translated in the year 181 BC.

There are two other early copies of the common version of Esther found in the Codex Vaticanus, the copy in the Codex Sinaiticus from circa 350 AD, and Codex Alexandrinus from circa 450 AD. The next oldest version of Esther that survives is in the Aleppo Codex of the Masoretic Text, which is dated to circa 920 AD. This version is in Hebrew, and is the only one of the three copies that does not appear to have once been in Greek, and it is the only one of the three copies that does not mention God. This version was copied as part of the Masoretic Text between the 7th and 10th centuries AD. With many Masoretic Text, there are precursors found among the Dead Sea Scrolls, however, there are no known fragments of Esther found among the Dead Sea Scrolls to date. It is unclear where it originated, or why there is no reference to God in it.

The next oldest physical copy that survives to the present is the Alpha Text version found in the Septuagint manuscript 319, which is dated to 1021 AD. The Alpha Texts version only survives in a few copies of the Septuagint, and based on its dialect, it was translated somewhere in the Seleucid Empire. The Alpha version is probably the oldest of the four translations, as it includes several unique elements that appear to have disappeared in later translations. One of these unique elements is the use of the month name Adar-Nisan (Αδάρ Νισα), which is then clarified in a scribal note as being Dystros-Xandicos (Δύστροσ Ξανδικόσ). Dystros-Xandicos was not a month, but two months on the modified Macedonian calendar used by the Seleucid Empire. As the story is set in the Persian Empire, the calendar in use was either the Persian calendar, or the Babylonian calendar. The names are the same as the Hebrew calendar, which are themselves based on the Babylonian Calendar, suggesting that this was the calendar the author used.

The Alpha texts version the month, 'Adar-Nisan' (which is 'Dystros Xandicos,') is a curiosity. Adar-Nisan is not a month, however, may be an archaic attempt to refer to Ådar B (אדר ב'), the second month of Adar that falls between Ådar Å (אדר א') and Nisan in leap years. The Hebrew calendar was derived from the Babylonian calendar, which was itself a descendant of the Akkadian calendar, which in turn was descended from the Sumerian calendar used in Ur. It is a lunisolar calendar, with 12 lunar months each year, and an additional intercalary month every two or three years, for a total of seven leap years every 19 years.

The calendar was in use among the various nations of Mesopotamia since at least the 3rd millennium BC, however, it is believed the intercalary month was added during the Old Babylonian Empire, in the early 2nd millennium BC. The Hebrew name Nisan is derived from the Akkadian Nissan (𒀭). The Sumerians had previously called the month Bar (𒁇). The Hebrew name Adar is likewise derived from the Akkadian Addari (𒊺), which the Sumerians likely pronounced as She (𒊺). This second month of Adar was established in the Babylonian calendar long before the Judahites were taken captive by Nebuchadnezzar, and was called Addaru Arku (𒊺𒀳). It is unclear what the Judahites would have called it in the early Persian era when the book is set.

If this strange month name of Adar-Nisan was in the original Aramaic text, and referred to the second month of Adar, directly before Nisan, then its removal from subsequent translations makes sense, as the Egyptian Greeks and Latins did not use an intercalary month, and would not have known what this term referred to. It is worth noting that the years with these strange months reported in the Alpha Texts version of Esther all correlate with leap years on the old Babylonian calendar, assuming the king in the book was Xerxes I, which would have been 485 BC and 474 BC. While the history of the Alpha Texts' version of Esther isn't clear, the origin does appear to be somewhere in the Seleucid Empire, before Ptolemy III standardized the Macedonian calendar in 247 BC, after which the intercalary month became Dystros II (Δύστρος Β).

The Vetus Latina is accepted as having been translated by 200 AD, based on the many quotes of it by early Christians, however, continued in use alongside the Vulgate in the Catholic countries until the 1300s. While the Vetus Latina is by nature a Latin translation of the ancient scriptures, the translations were made from the Greek translations, and in the case of the Book of Esther, not from either the Vaticanus or Alpha versions. The Vetus Latina version of Esther contains specific references that prove it was originally a Greek translation, including the scribal note that clarifies that the month of Nisan in the text was the month of Andicus, which was the Latin translation of Xanthicos (Ξανθικός) on the

Macedonian calendar. The Macedonian calendar was the official calendar of Alexander's Empire and was continued in the Seleucid Empire after he died. In Egypt, the Ptolemys adopted the Egyptian Civil Calendar, and renamed the Egyptian months the names of months found in the Athenian calendar. This, therefore, proves that the original Greek source text for the Vetus Latina, was translated in either Alexander's Empire, or the subsequent Seleucid Empire. As the Vetus Latina is missing references to the month of Adar-Nisan, it is likely it was translated into Greek sometime after 247 BC.

The Vetus Latina version of Esther includes several structural and theological differences from the other three copies of Esther. The biggest theological difference is that more of the actions in the book are attributed to Mordecai, instead of other people in the king's court, and Mordecai being a prophet. The Rabbinical tradition has never recognized Mordecai as a prophet, although Esther is considered a prophet. The Vetus Latina also includes a reference to the God of Abraham, Isaac, and Jacob, which was likely added when the book was translated into Greek. This reference to the God of Abraham, Isaac, and Jacob, was far more common among the Israelite priesthoods that Ezra had ejected from the Second Temple in

351 BC. Many of these other Israelites lived in the region around Damascus, and had since the time of David.

During the wars between the Ptolemys and Seleucids, many escaped the fighting by fleeing to Egypt, while others were forcibly relocated to Egypt, and therefore a large Israelite community existed in southern Egypt by 200 BC. These Israelites were mostly driven out of Egypt in 200 BC when the province of Judea rebelled against the rule of Ptolemy's Egypt. This means the original Greek translation of the Vetus Latina version, was likely made in the 3rd century BC, somewhere in southern Syria, before being carried to Egypt. The Testaments of Abraham, Isaac, and Jacob continued to be used by the Beta Israel and Beta Abraham communities in Sudan and Ethiopia, however, the version of Esther adopted by the Ethiopian Tewahedo Church was the Vaticanus version, which is believed to have been translated from the Greek. While the Vetus Latina version, or one like it, was used in Egypt, it is unclear if the Beta Abraham community continues to use a version of Esther.

Fragments of either a Greek copy of the Vetus Latina, or a fifth version of Esther, were discovered among the Oxyrhynchus Papyri (LXV 4443 / LXX 996) in Egypt, and are dated to circa 100 AD. Unfortunately, the LXV 4443 version is missing most of Esther, and includes only fragments of chapter 6 and 7. Scholars debate the amount of similarity there is between LXV 4443 and the Vetus Latina version of Esther, however, it is generally agreed that the Vetus Latina is the closest surviving version of Esther to the LXV 4443 papyrus.

The Vaticanus, Alpha Texts, and Vetus Latina versions all include the curious reference to the 'king of the gods,' 'Lord God King,' and the title 'Lord King' for God. The term 'king of the gods' (βασιλευ των θεων) is found in chapter 4 of the Vaticanus version of Esther, however, does not make sense in the theology that developed in later Judaism, in which there was only one God, indicating the early date of the original composition. The title 'king of the gods' was used by Esther in the book, who use the title to refer to the god of the Israelites. While Esther was described as being the Queen (or royal consort) in the texts, she was also described as being a devoted worshiper of the Israelite god, and 'King of the gods' was not a Zoroastrian title of Ahura Mazda either, as Zoroastrianism was also monotheistic, meaning that this title has to be traced back to the Israelite religion.

Her uncle Mordecai also made references that support their god as being named 'King,' including the terms Lord King (Κύριε Βασιλευ) and Lord God King (Κύριε ο θεὸς ο βασιλεὺς) in the Vaticanus version, and Lord King

(Κύριε Βασιλευ / Dominus Rex) in the Alpha and Vetus Latina version. These names can only indicate that Mordecai and Esther were worshipers of the ancient Canaanite, Moabite, and early-Israelite god Moloch. The Greek and Latin terms can only be translated back into Aramaic as Lord Melech (ᚦᛏᚦᚾ ᚾᛃᛚᚦ) or Lord God Melech (ᚾᛃᛚᚦ ᛚᚾ ᚦᛏᚦᚾ). The use of the name Melech (ᚾᛃᛚᚦ) renders the name as Moloch, which was a proper name of a god, that happened to be spelled the same way as the word for 'king' in Aramaic (ᚾᛃᛚᚦ), Hebrew (מֶלֶךְ), Canaanite (𐤌𐤋𐤊), and Syriac (ܡܠܟܐ).

That the Judahites were worshiping a god named Moloch is not debated, King Josiah banned Moloch's worship in 625 BC, when he promoted Yhwh to be the Judahite national god, however, based on the writings of Baruch, it is clear that the Judahites reverted to the old gods after Josiah died. This also explains why the Masoretic version had all references to God stripped from it, as the book was about a prophet of the wrong god. The additions of the set of names 'Abraham, Isaac, and Jacob,' found in the Vetus Latina version also makes sense, as the translators seem to have been trying to justify Moloch by stating he was the god of the three ancient patriarchs. The Judahites and Israelites in southern Egypt never stopped using the name Moloch, and carried it south with them into Sudan and Ethiopia, and the Ge'ez (and Amharic) word for 'God' continues to be Åämlak (አምላክ) to this day, derived from the ancient Semitic word for king.

The setting of the book is also an issue that has been debated over the centuries. The king in the story is called Artaxerxes (Αρταξέρξου) in the Vaticanus version, but Ahasuerus (אֲחַשְׁוֵרוֹשׁ / Ασσερος / Asuerus) in the Masoretic, Alpha, and Vetus Latina versions of the book. The name Ahasuerus is not the proper translation of Artaxerxes, but of Xerxes, and most modern scholars believe the classical translation of Artaxerxes was an error. Additional ancient sources for the Book of Esther exist, including Josephus' version from the late 1st century AD, and three major targums dating to between 500 and 1000 AD: the Targum Rishon, Targum Sheni, and Targum Shelishi.

Josephus claimed that Artaxerxes was the Greek translation of Ahasuerus, a view repeated in Josippon in the late 10th century, and the Esther Rabbah in the late 11th century, nevertheless, it is not actually correct, as the Greek name Xerxes (Ξέρξης) and Hebrew name Ahasuerus (אחשורוש), both derive from the Old Persian Xshaya-ṛsha (𐎧𐏁𐎹𐎠𐎼𐏁𐎠). The Greek is derived directly from the Persian, while the Hebrew is derived from the Babylonian Aḫshiyarshu (𒄴𒅆𒅀𒅈𒋗). As the Vaticanus version of Esther was likely translated around

181 BC, and in Jerusalem, it is even less likely that the translator would have known the origin of the various names of the Persian kings, and likely just picked the Greek name that was the most similar-sounding to the name in the Aramaic texts that was being translated.

There were four Persian kings name Artaxerxes: Artaxerxes I who reigned between 465 and 424 BC, Artaxerxes II Mnemon who reigned between 404 and 358 BC, Artaxerxes III Ochus who reigned between 358 and 338 BC, and Artaxerxes IV Arses who reigned between 338 and 336 BC. There were two Persian kings named Xerxes: Xerxes I who reigned between 486 and 465 BC, and Xerxes II who reigned for 45 days in 424 BC. The Vaticanus, Vetus Latina, and Masoretic versions of Esther all refer to the 12th year of Artaxerxes/ Ahasuerus reign removing the possibility of this king being either Artaxerxes IV Arses or Xerxes II, neither of which ruled for 12 years. Three of the source texts also mention that he ruled from India (Sindhu) to Kush (Aethiopia), which also reduces the number of possible kings, as Artaxerxes II never ruled Egypt. Egypt had broken away when he assumed the throne, and remained independent for 60 years until Artaxerxes III reconquered them in 343 BC, ten years before Alexander conquered Egypt into his Macedonian Empire. This leaves the kings Xerxes I, Artaxerxes I, and Artaxerxes III as the possible kings of the Book of Esther.

There are many indicators in the story, that point to it being set in the era of Xerxes I, the first of which is the reference to him calling all the satraps (governors) of Persia to the capital of Susa in his third year. Both the Vaticanus and Masoretic versions of Esther agree that it was the third year, while the Vetus Latina reports it was in the twelfth year. As the years in the Vetus Latina are out of order, as the events in the seventh year follow the events of the twelfth, the chronology of the Vetus Latina is suspect, and therefore most scholars accept that the original year referenced by the author was regal year 3 of the king's reign. In the case of Xerxes I, this was 483 BC, when Xerxes did call his satraps to Susa to plan the invasion of Greece.

The invasion took years of planning and involved building two bridges across the Hellespont to allow for easy troop movements from Anatolia to the Balkans, and the Xerxes Canal was dug through the isthmus of the Mount Athos peninsula. A massive army from across the empire was raised, including Achaean Greeks, Aegean Greeks, Aeolian Greeks, Assyrians, Babylonians, Black Sea Greeks, Colchians, Egyptians, Indians, Ionian Greeks, Judeans, Macedonians, Paeonians, Phoenicians, and Thracians. It took around three years for the invasion force to be mobilized, and they set out in 480 BC. Therefore, the description of Xerxes I calling his satraps to the capital in 483 BC makes sense. The war was short, and Xerxes negotiated a treaty with the Greeks, following which he did not launch any major wars, and instead focused on construction projects, including the Palace of Darius in Susa, which is likely where most of this story was set. Susa was reported to be the favorite capital of Darius I, which was why he built the Palace. Xerxes then greatly expanded it after returning from Greece. Later Persian kings also expanded the Palace, including Artaxerxes I, Darius II, and Artaxerxes II.

In comparison, when Artaxerxes I assumed the throne, in 465 BC, Egypt revolted, and he was not able to restore control until 454 BC, his eleventh year, and therefore, did not call all the satraps to the capital in his third year. In Artaxerxes III's second year, 356 BC, he attempted to dismiss Artabazus II from his satrapy of Hellespontine Phrygia, and Artabazus started a rebellion that did not end until 354 BC, Artaxerxes III's fourth year. Therefore, Artaxerxes III would not have called the satraps to the capital in his third year either. During those rebellions, the last thing the king would want is all the satraps in the same place where they could conspire against him.

FORWARD

The Vaticanus, Masoretic, and Vetus Latina versions of Esther all also tell a story set in Susa during the king's seventh year. If this was King Xerxes I, then this would have been the year 479 BC. At the time Xerxes was still engaged in his major construction projects across the empire, including the expansions of the Palace of Darius in Susa, where the story is set. However, during King Artaxerxes I's seventh year, 458 BC, Artaxerxes I's was still engaged in his attempt to reconquer Egypt, and is not believed to have visited Susa. Likewise, in Artaxerxes III's seventh year, 351 BC, he launched his first campaign to reconquer Egypt, and it was a complete failure, leading to the satraps across Anatolia, Cyprus, and Phoenicia declaring independence, and it is believed he did not return to Susa until sometime in 350 BC, meaning this story is almost certainly not about him.

The antagonist of Mordecai was Haman (Αμαν / הָמָן), which is a name found in the records of the Persian court as Imanish (𐎡𐎶𐎴𐎡𐏁) from the era of Darius I and Xerxes I. Haman was recorded as being the son of Amadathou (Αμαδαθου) in the Vaticanus and Alpha versions, Hammedoso (הַמְּדָתָא) in the Masoretic version, and Medadatum in the Vetus Latina. This person called a Bougaeos (Βουγαιος) in both the Vaticanus and Alpha versions, a Macedonian (Μακεδών/Macedonica) in the Vaticanus, Alpha, and Vetus Latina versions, and an

17

Agagai (אֲגָגִי) in the Masoretic text. These terms are used interchangeably throughout the texts, meaning that whatever the original author had in mind, the Greek translators accepted the words in the Aramaic source texts as all referring to Macedonia.

The Greek term Bougaeos is an unknown term, and used as a proper name in the texts, however, is similar to another rare Greek word that translates as bully or braggart, and is often translated that way. As it is used as a substitute for Macedonian in both places, it is likely an attempt to transliterate Brygoe (Βρύγοι) back into Greek from Aramaic. The Brygoe, more commonly called the Bryges in English, were a tribe of people that settled in Macedonia, northern Greece, and Albania shortly before the Persians invaded Greece.

The term used in the Masoretic version is generally accepted as the name of a tribe, and is often assumed to be descended from the ancient Amalekite king Agag from the time of King Saul. An alternate theory is that Agagai (אֲגָגִי) is a reference to Aigai (Αἰγαὶ), the capital of Macedonia before 399 BC. This was clearly the way the translators of the other versions interpreted the word, resulting in the term Macedonians. All three sources other than the Masoretic version, include a letter that refers to Haman as involved in a Macedonian plot to destabilize the Persian Empire. Clearly, the translator of the Vaticanus version did not want to offend the monarchs he was preparing the translation for, and so transliterated the word Bougaeos instead of translating it in sections of text where the Macedonian was being praised.

It is worth noting that early in his reign, Ptolemy V had fought a major war against the Macedonians, and lost. Mentioning them in the book the translator was preparing for Ptolemy V and Cleopatra I would have not been well received, which would explain why he transliterated the word instead of translating it as Macedonian.

At the beginning of Xerxes I's reign, Macedonia was a district of the Persian Empire, although it regained its independence after Xerxes' failed invasion of the Greek mainland. Xerxes I had inherited the Persian Empire from Darius I at its greatest extent. It is not clear how much of the world was considered under Persian rule at the time, as Darius had campaigned in Egypt, India, and Greece. He even attempted to conquer the Scythians and marched his army through the Balkans, and east around the Black Sea before capturing Crimea. The Scythian King Idanthyrsus was not willing to face the Persian army in open combat, and so Darius built a series of forts on the Oarus River (Volga River) to mark the new boundary of his empire, and returned to the Bosporus.

The location of the Oarus River is debated somewhat, however, the dominant modern view is that it is the Volga. The ancient Scythian name for the Volga was the Rha, while the ancient Finnic name was Rau, and Herodotus, who lived around the same time (484-425 BC), reported that the Oarus River flowed through the land of the Scythian Thyssagetae tribe, who lived seven days journey east across the desert from the Scythian Budini tribe, a tribe reported to have lived in the region of the Tanis River (modern Don River).

This has been debated somewhat as Herodotus also reported that the Oarus flowed into the Maeotis (modern Sea of Azov), however, this could easily have arisen due to confusion over the Don-Volga-Portage, which was a major overland route connecting the two rivers from sometime in the first millennium BC to 1952, when the Soviets opened the Volga-Don Canal. Archaeological evidence supports it as having been used since before 438 BC, when the Bosporan Kingdom formed to control the route, and so when Herodotus was writing, the trade from the Volga was flowing into the Sea of Azov, even if the Volga River was not.

While the exact location of the Oarus River is occasionally debated today, it was known in Herodotus time, as Darius' fortresses were still there. Herodotus reported that when Darius's army reached the desert, he built a series of eight forts, each 60 stadia apart, at the Oarus River. This is often assumed to be a series of forts along the Oarus, to serve as a frontier, however, the geography is self-contradicting, as Herodotus placed the river on the other side of the desert. This appears to be a description of Darius attempting to secure the Volga-Don-Portage, which was around 70 kilometers (43.5 miles) long.

The Greek stadion that Herodotus used, he also defined as being 600 feet long. The length of the foot is not consistent, and so Greek lands used slightly different lengths of a stadion, and modern estimates of various Greek stadia in use, range from 157 meters (172 yards) to 185 meters (202 yards). Therefore eight forts 60 stadia apart would be a length of between 75 kilometers (46.6 miles) and 89 kilometers (55.3 miles). The series of forts are otherwise a strange anomaly in a never-ending steppe that the Scythians could have easily gone around. Clearly, they were strategically placed along a 75 to 90 kilometer-long route, and therefore it seems clear the forts ran through the desert, and Darius was attempting to secure the road to the Volga, most likely in order to tax the goods traveling through the region.

Apparently, the Persians did not consider the Caucasus Mountains safe to travel through and so took the longer route back to the empire in Thrace. The region was listed as a subject land of the Persian Empire, Sakha

Yayaiya Paradraya (𒅀𒅀𒁹𒈬𒀖𒈨𒀖𒁹𒌋𒈨𒀖), meaning 'Scythia across the Sea,' meaning that while he could not find the Scythian army to defeat in battle, Darius did consider his campaign successful.

During Darius I's march north into the Balkans, he had subjugated the Persian vassal kingdom of Macedon, which had been ruled by King Amyntas (Αμύντας). Amyntas continued to be referred to as a king until he died in 498 BC, after which his heir, Alexander I was referred to by the title of hyparchos (under-satrap) until after the Persians were driven out by the Greeks after Xerxes I failed invasion of 480 BC. The reference to Haman's father Amadathou / Hammedoso appears to be a reference to King Amyntas, translated from Greek to Aramaic, and then back into Greek or into Hebrew, which would then make Haman a Macedonian prince in the Persian court, the brother of Alexander I in the era the story takes place. This reading is equally valid whether the king in the story is Xerxes I, or his son Artaxerxes I, however, the chronology makes more sense in the era of Xerxes I.

Haman is first mentioned in regal year 2 of the king's reign, as being angry after Mordecai foiled a plot by two eunuchs to kill the king. As this event would date to 484 BC if the king was Xerxes I, the events are likely related to revolts in Babylonia that year. In the summer of 484 BC, two Babylonians led revolts against Persian rule. Shamash-eriba was recognized as king in the city of Sippar, in northern Babylonia, and within weeks Bel-shimanni was recognized as king in the towns of Borsippa and Dilbat in southern Babylonia. Bel-shimanni's revolt only lasted a few weeks, however, Shamash-eriba's revolt wasn't crushed until the following spring. As the assassination plot of the two eunuchs must have been related to either another monarch seizing the throne, or a rebellion within the empire, this timing does correlate with what was happening in the Persian Empire in Xerxes I's second year. Haman was reported as being angry that Mordecai had stopped the plot to kill the king, which later resurfaced after the events of year 7.

Year 7 of Xerxes reign, was 479 BC, the year the Persian army returned from the failed invasion of Greece. Macedonia had gone from being a district of the empire to being an independent kingdom, and the most valuable ally of Persia in Greece. Therefore, the reference to Haman being elevated above everyone else in year 7 makes sense if he was Amyntas I's son, and his brother Alexander I was the king of Macedonia. Alexander I continued to be the king of Macedonia well into the subsequent reign of Artaxerxes I, however, was no longer an ally by that point. Conversely, there is no way to correlate the reference to a Macedonian prince in the Persian court in the era of Artaxerxes III, nor was Aigai the capital of Macedonia after 399 BC, so the Masoretic reference to it would have been anachronistic.

The climax of the story takes place in year 12 of the king, in which Haman is ultimately accused of attempting to cause disorder within the Persian Empire as part of a plot for the Macedonians to take over. Haman and his entire family are executed, as are many others across the empire. This event would have taken place in 474 BC, one year after the Greeks captured the garrisoned port city of Eion that the Persians had left on the Macedonian coast when Xerxes withdrew his forces after the failed attempt to conquer Greece in 480 and 479 BC. After Eion fell, the only Persian garrison in Europe was at Doriscus near the Hellespont, which had been founded by Darius I when he invaded the Balkans during the Scythian War. This outpost was also abandoned when Xerxes I died in 465 BC, in an attempt to make peace with the Greeks. Nevertheless, in King Xerxes I's twelfth year, 474 BC, Macedonia had suddenly become irrelevant to the Persian position in the Balkans, and a year later Haman was accused of plotting against the empire, and executed.

The general modern view is that the king in Esther is Xerxes I, as many of the names in the story are attested in his court, however, the story itself is generally considered fiction. This would place the events of the story between 484 and 478 BC. While the identification of King Ahasuerus with Xerxes I, and Haman with the person known as Imanish in the Persian records from the time is fairly accepted, the identification of Amadathou the Macedonian as the King Amyntas I of Macedonia continues to be debated as many scholars have no interest in studying any version of Esther other than the Masoretic version, which is itself the one with the most mysterious origin, and likely the last translation made from the Aramaic source text.

If the king was Xerxes I, then the original queen in the text was his wife Amastri. This name does not survive in the source texts, which instead use the name Astin (Αστιν), Ouastin (Ουαστιν), and Vashti (וַשְׁתִּי), however, as the Greek and Hebrew translators did not recognize the Aramaic name Ahasuerus as referring to Xerxes, it is unlikely they'd recognize his wife's name either. Queen Amastri was known in Greek records from the era as Amestris (Ἀμηστρις), Ámāstris (Ἀμαστρις), or Amastrinē (Ἀμαστρινε).

Xerxes I was already married to Amastri before Darius I died. It had been a political wedding, as her father Otanes had been one of the seven Persians that helped Xerxes I kill his predecessor King Bardiya (or a magical doppelganger named Gaumata) and seize the Persian throne. She lived a long time, and is believed to have died in 424 BC, probably at more than 80 years old. The ancient Greeks accused her of making human sacrifices to Hades in order to live so long, however, there is no evidence of human sacrifice in the Persian Empire, and Persian law expressly forbade it.

In the story of Esther, the king got mad at his wife while he was drunk one night, because she was not obedient enough, and was advised to take another wife. According to the Book of Esther, Esther then became the king's new queen four years later. There is no evidence that Xerxes had ever divorced Amastri, and this would have been contrary to Persian custom and law at the time, as well as the teachings of the Zoroastrian religion at the time. The Persian custom at the time, much like today, was polygamy, in which Persian men could marry multiple wives, but were financially responsible for all of them and their children. Xerxes I is known to have taken wives other than Amastri, however, their names have not survived to the present, and so the historical core of the story in Esther cannot be disproved. The story is, nevertheless, widely considered as fiction, by Jewish, Christian, and secular scholars, primarily as Esther's name has not been documented in ancient Persian records as being a wife of Xerxes I.

Whatever the source of the various versions of the Book of Esther, the version presented to Ptolemy and Cleopatra was ultimately added to the Septuagint sometime before 132 BC. This was a tumultuous time in the history of Judea. In 200 BC, the Greek Kingdom of Syria under the Seleucid Dynasty took Judea from Egypt, and began an effort to Hellenize the Judeans, which included erecting a statue of Zeus in the Second Temple in Jerusalem, and effectively banning traditional Judaism. This Hellenizing activity was partially successful, creating the Sadducee faction of Judaism, however, it also led to the Maccabean Revolt in 165 BC, which itself created the independent Kingdom of Judea. This Kingdom had a tenuous alliance with the Roman Republic until General Pompey conquered Syria into the Roman Republic in 69 BC. Pompey's goal was to liberate Greek-speaking communities in the Middle East that had fallen under the rule of non-Greeks when the Seleucids Syrian Empire had collapsed, and he carved up Judea, and Edom to the southeast, placing Greek-speaking cities under the protection of the Roman province of Syria. He also liberated several smaller communities that had been occupied by Judea, granting them self-government, including Ashdod, Yavne, Jaffa, Dora, Marissa, and Samaria.

FORWARD

A series of wars including both Julius Caesar's campaigns, and a Parthian invasion led to the weakening of the Hasmonean dynasty, and in 37 AD, the Roman Senate appointed Herod the Great as king of Judea. Herod's rule wasn't particularly popular, as he allowed the Romans to establish themselves within Judea, however, he did expand Judea, reintegrating the Greek and Samaritan cities, and annexing Galilee and Edom. When he died, his kingdom was divided between four successors, a situation that ended in 66 AD when the Romans conquered the region. An uprising in 120 AD led to the Jews being exiled from Judea, and the region became a Greco-Roman colony. In the wake of the Jews, the Samaritans rose in numbers, along with the Christians once Christianity was legalized. Between 529 and 555 AD, the Samaritans revolted and were effectively annihilated, by the Byzantine Empire.

Outside of Judea, the Septuagint was the dominant form of Jewish scriptures across the Greek-speaking world, which by the beginning of the Christian era extended from the Roman Empire in the west, to the Indo-Greek Kingdom in the east. Jewish traders had established small colonies along the trade routes of the Red Sea and the Indian Ocean, reaching as far south as Yemen, and as far east as southern India, and these Jews spoke Greek and used the Septuagint.

The earliest Christian Bibles, all used the Septuagint, however, by the 4th century some Christian scholars were debating whether they should retranslate the Old Testament from the version the Jews were using, and some even suggested using the Samaritan version. Both suggestions were generally dismissed as heretical, as Jesus and the Apostles had quoted from the Septuagint, even though they had access to the Hebrew version then in use. This argument held in the west until the Middle Ages, when Catholic Bibles switched to the Masoretic Text. In the east, Orthodox Bibles continued to use the Septuagint, as they do today. To the south, the Ethiopian Tewahedo Church continued to use the Septuagint, and across Asia, the Thomas Christians and Nestorians continued to use the Septuagint. Only in Western Europe were the later Masoretic Text adopted, abandoning the more ancient Septuagint, on the assumption that the Jews had copied their texts more faithfully than the Greeks had translated them. This assumption carried forward into the Protestant Churches that broke off from the Catholic Church, and therefore almost all Protestant Bibles use the Masoretic Text for the basis of the Old Testament.

Unfortunately, this means that the earliest Christian writing is generally confusing and ignored by Protestants and Catholics. The earliest Christians of the first and second centuries quoted books that are no longer in the Bible, and as such, their writings are not always understood. Septuagint: Esther is a 21st century translation aimed at correcting this problem.

One of the problems with academic translations of the Septuagint, is the use of unfamiliar names or terms, as the Septuagint was written in Greek, and therefore many names are unrecognizable to modern English readers who are used to Hebrew-derived names. This project uses the more commonly understood Hebrew-derived names instead of their Greek translations, such as Canaan instead of Chanaan, and Melchizedek instead of Melchisedec. Common modern names are also used instead of either Greek or Hebrew terms when geographical locations are known, such as the archaeological name Uruk instead of the Greek Orech, or the Hebrew Erech, and the archaeological term Sumer instead of Shinar or Senar. While this could be argued as not being a correct academic procedure, it does fulfill the goal of making the translation easy to read and understand.

Esther (Vaticanus): Chapter 1

In the second year of the reign of Artaxerxes[1] the great king, on the first day of Nisan,[2] Mordecai[3] the son of Jair the son of Shimei the son of Kish,[4] of the tribe of Benjamin, a Judahite[5] living in Susa, the capital city,[6] a great man serving in the king's palace, saw a vision. He was of the captives which King Nebuchadnezzar[7] of Babylon had taken captive from Jerusalem, with King Jeconiah[8] of Judah, and this was his dream.

There was noise and an uproar, thunder and earthquake, and trouble on the land. Then two great dragons[9] came out ready to fight, and from them came a great call, and by their call every nation was prepared for the battle to make war against the lawful people.[10] A day of gloom and darkness, sorrow and sadness, injury and great trouble on the land. All the lawful people were troubled, fearing the other's evil, and they were prepared to be destroyed and shouted to God,[11] and as if from a small fountain came many great rivers of waters. Light[12] and the Sun[13] rose, and the lowly were exalted and devoured the honorable.

After Mordecai had seen this dream and what God desired to do, and having woken up, he thought about it and tried to interpret every detail until nightfall. Then Mordecai rested in the courtyard, which was guarded by Gabatha[14] and Teresh,[15] the king's two eunuchs,[16] when he overheard their plotting and deliberating, and he found out that they were preparing to capture King Artaxerxes, and he told the king their plans. The king interrogated the two eunuchs, and they confessed and were led away.

The king inscribed these events in the records,[17] and also Mordecai wrote about these matters. The king commanded Mordecai to visit him in the palace and gave gifts for this service.

Haman[18] the son of Amyntas[19] the Bryge[20] was honorable in the sight of the king, and he later endeavored to hurt Mordecai and his people because of what happened with the two eunuchs of the king.

After these things, in the days of Artaxerxes (this is the Artaxerxes who controlled 127 lands from India),[21] when king Artaxerxes was on the throne in the city of Susa, in the third year of his reign,[22] he held a feast for his friends, and the other nations, and to the nobles of the Persians and Medes, and the rulers of the satrapies.[23]

After he had shown the wealth of his kingdom to them, and the abundant glory of his wealth over 180 days, and when the days of the marriage feast were completed, the king made a banquet to the nations who were present in the city for six days, in the court of the king's house, which was adorned with drapes of cotton and flax on cords of fine linen and purple, fastened to golden and silver studs, on pillars of Parian[24] marble and stone. There were golden and silver couches on a pavement of emerald stone, and of pearl, and of Parian marble, and decorated with beds of bright flowers of various colors, with roses around them. There were gold and silver cups, and a small cup of carbuncle valued at thirty thousand talents, and a large amount of sweet wine, which the king himself drank.

This banquet was not appointed by the law, but because the king ordered it, and he ordered the stewards to perform his will and that of the company. Additionally, Queen Astin[25] made a banquet for the women in the palace where king Artaxerxes lived.

On the seventh day, the king, while the king was drunk, told the seven eunuchs Aman, Bazan, Tharrha, Boraze, Zatholtha, Abataza, and Tharaba,[26] his servants, to bring the queen to him, to enthrone her, and crown her with the diadem, and to show her beauty to the princes of the nations, for she was very beautiful. However, Queen Astin did not listen to him to accompany the eunuchs, so the king was grieved and angered.

He said to his friends, "Astin has said this, judge this case by the law."

Then Arcesaeos, Sarsathaeos, and Malesear,[27] the princes of the Persians and Medes, who were near the king, who sat first in rank next to the king, approached him and reported according to the laws what it was proper to do to Queen Astin, because she had not done the things commanded of the king through his eunuchs. Mouchaeos[28] said to the king and to the princes, "Queen Astin has not just wronged the king, but also all the king's governors and princes, for he has told them the words of the queen, and how she disobeyed the king. She refused to obey King Artaxerxes, from this day onward the other ladies of the chiefs of the Persians and Medes, having heard what she said to the king, will dare in the same way to disobey their husbands. If then it seems good to the king, let him make a royal decree, and let it be written according to the laws of the Medes and Persians, and let him not alter it. Don't let the queen come into his presence again, and let the king give her royalty to a woman more deserving than she. Let the law of the king which he will have made, be widely proclaimed in his kingdom, and so will all the women obey their husbands, from the poor even to the rich."

The words pleased the king and the princes, and the king did as Mouchaeos had said, and sent throughout all his kingdom, and through the many provinces, according to their language, so that men should be obeyed in their own houses.

Esther (Vaticanus): Chapter 1 Notes

1 Codex Vaticanus: Artaxérxou (ΑΡΤΑΞΕΡΞΟΥ).
Translation: Artaxerxes

• Septuagint manuscript 319: Assyeros (Ασσύβος).
Translation: Ahasuerus (or Xerxes)

• Aleppo Codex: Åḥšwrwš (אַחַשְׁוֵרוֹשׁ). Translation:
Ahasuerus (or Xerxes)

• Leningrad Codex: Achashverosh (אֲחַשְׁוֵרוֹשׁ). Translation:
Ahasuerus (or Xerxes)

• Codex Monacensis (VL 130): Asueri. Translation:
Ahasuerus (or Xerxes)

The debate regarding who the king in the book of Esther is, goes back to before the Vaticanus version was translated in Jerusalem. The Codex Vaticanus is the primary source that names the king Artaxerxes, however, the other sources name the king Ahasuerus. Josephus in the late 1st century AD claimed that Artaxerxes (Αρταξέρξου) was the Greek translation of Åḥšwrwš (אַחַשְׁוֵרוֹשׁ), a view repeated in Josippon in the late 10th century, and the Esther Rabbah in the late 11th century, nevertheless, it is not actually correct, as the Greek name Xerxes (Ξέρξης) and Hebrew name Åḥšwrwš (אַחַשְׁוֵרוֹשׁ), both derive from the Old Persian Xshaya-rsha (𐎧𐏁𐎹𐎠𐎼𐏁𐎠). The Greek is derived directly from the Persian, while the Hebrew is derived from the Babylonian Aḥshiyarshu (𒄴𒅆𒐊𒅈𒋗). As the Vaticanus version of Esther was likely translated around 181 BC, and in Jerusalem, it is even less likely that the translator would have known the origin of the various names of the Persian

36

kings, and likely just picked the Greek name that was the most similar-sounding to the name in the Aramaic texts that were being translated.

There were four Persian kings name Artaxerxes: Artaxerxes I who reigned between 465 and 424 BC, Artaxerxes II Mnemon who reigned between 404 and 358 BC, Artaxerxes III Ochus who reigned between 358 and 338 BC, and Artaxerxes IV Arses who reigned between 338 and 336 BC. There were two Persian kings named Xerxes: Xerxes I who reigned between 486 and 465 BC, and Xerxes II who reigned for 45 days in 424 BC.

The Vaticanus, Vetus Latina, and Masoretic versions of Esther all refer to the 12th year of Artaxerxes/Ahasuerus reign removing the possibility of this king being either Artaxerxes IV Arses or Xerxes II, neither of which ruled for 12 years. Three of the source texts also mention that he ruled from India (Sindhu) to Kush (Aethiopia), which further reduces the number of possible kings, as Artaxerxes II never ruled Egypt, it had broken away when he assumed the throne, and remained independent for 60 years until Artaxerxes III reconquered them in 343 BC, ten years before Alexander conquered Egypt into his Macedonian Empire. This leaves the kings Xerxes I, Artaxerxes I, and Artaxerxes III as the possible kings of the Book of Esther.

The general modern view is that the king in Esther is Xerxes I, as many of the names in the story are attested in his court, however, the story itself is generally considered fiction. This would place the events of the story between 484 and 474 BC. He had inherited the Persian Empire from Darius I at its greatest extent. It is not clear how much of the world was considered under Persian rule at the time, as Darius had campaigned in Egypt, India, and Greece. He even attempted to conquer the Scythians, and marched his army into the Balkans, and then north around the Black Sea before capturing Crimea.

The Vaticanus version of Esther specifically names the king in the book Artaxerxes, however, the other source texts agree that this was Ahasuerus (אחשורוש / Ασσερος / Asuerus), not Artaxerxes (Αρταξέρξου). As the name Artaxerxes appears to have been adopted in the Classical era by translators due to its phonetic similarity to Ahasuerus.

2 Codex Vaticanus: Nisa (ⲚⲓⳞⲁ). Translation: Nisan

• Septuagint manuscript 319: Adar Nisa (ⲀⲆⲁⲱⲛⳞ Ⲛⲓⲥⲁ). Translation: Adar-Nisan

• Masoretic Text: section missing

• Codex Monacensis (VL 130): Nisan

The month of Nîsān (נִיסָן) is the first month of the ecclesiastical year in the Hebrew calendar. It happens during March and April in the Gregorian Calendar. The name of the month, like the rest of the calendar, was adopted by the Judahites during the Babylonian captivity. In Neo-Babylonian the month was known as Nisānu (𒌷𒁇), and the name was in use since at least the second millennium BC. In the Torah, which predates the Babylonian captivity, the month was known as åbyb (אביב), its old Canaanite name. The Book of Esther is the earliest Judahite work that uses the name Nisan, although it did become the common name of the month in the Babylonian Talmud, which was written in Babylonian Aramaic

The reference to Adar Nisa (Αδάρ Νισα) found in the Alpha Texts is odd. The Alpha Texts then has a scribal note added by the translator clarifying that this is the month of Dustros Xandicos (Δύστρος Ξανδικός). The Vetus Latina also has this scribal note, which clarifies that Nisan is the month of Andicus, which is a Latin transliteration of Xanthicos (Ξανθικός). Both Dustros (Δύστρος) and Xandicos (Ξανδικός) are names of months on the Macedonian calendar, which was the official calendar of Alexander's Empire, and was continued in the Seleucid Empire after he died. In Egypt, the Ptolemys adopted the Egyptian Civil Calendar, and renamed the Egyptian months the names of months found in the Athenian calendar. This, therefore, proves that the original Greek text of the Alpha Texts, as well as the Greek language source-text for the Vetus Latina, were both translated in either Alexander's Empire, or the subsequent Seleucid Empire.

The Alpha Text's version of the month, Adar Nisa (Αδάρ Νισα) which is Dustros Xandicos (Δύστρος Ξανδικός), is a curiosity. Adar Nisan is not a month, however, may be an archaic attempt to refer to Adar Bet (אדר ב'), the second month of Adar that falls between Adar Aleph (אדר א') and Nisan in leap years.

The Hebrew calendar was derived from the Babylonian calendar, which was itself a descendant of the Akkadian calendar, which in turn was descended from the Sumerian calendar used in Ur. It is a lunisolar calendar, with 12 lunar months each year, and an additional intercalary month every two or three years, for a total of seven leap years every 19 years. The calendar was in use among the various nations of Mesopotamia since at least the 3rd millennium BC, however, it is believed the intercalary month was added during the Old Babylonian Empire, in the early 2nd millennium BC. The Hebrew name Nisan is ultimately derived from the Akkadian Nissan (🔯). The Sumerians had previously called the month Bar (𒁇). The Hebrew name Adar is likewise derived from the Akkadian Addari (𒊺), which the Sumerians likely pronounced as She (𒊺). This second month of Adar was established in the Old Babylonian calendar long before the Judahites were taken captive by Nebuchadnezzar, and was called Addaru Arku (𒊺𒅅𒄀). It is unclear what the Judahites would have called it in the early Persian era, when the book it set.

If this strange month name of Adar-Nisan was in the original Aramaic text, and referred to the second month of Adar, directly before Nisan, then its removal from subsequent translations makes sense, as the Greeks and Latins did not use an intercalary month, and would not have known what this term referred to. If this is the case, then the Alpha version appears to be the oldest translation of Esther, and done within the Seleucid Empire. The Vetus Latina version of Esther, which is not standardized, also appears to be derived from a Greek translation made within the Seleucid Empire, but not the Alpha version. The Vaticanus version claims to have been translated in Jerusalem, however, is missing the strange name, and instead refers to Nisan (Νισα), which would make sense for a Judean translator in Jerusalem under Greek rule, as the text was being prepared for Ptolemy and Cleopatra, who would not have cared about whether it was a leap year or not.

It is worth noting that the year was reported in Esther was the second year of the king's reign, which would be 485 BC if this was Xerxes I, which was a leap year on the Old Babylonian calendar.

3 Codex Vaticanus: Mardochaeos (ΜΑΡΔΟΧΑΙΟC)

- Septuagint manuscript 319: Mardochaeos (ΜΑβΔοχΔιοc)

- Aleppo Codex (chapter 2): Mrdky (מרדכי)

- Leningrad Codex (chapter 2): Maredechai (מָרְדֳּכַי)

- Codex Monacensis (VL 130): Mardocheus

This name is believed to be a translation of the Neo-Babylonian name Marduka (⇒𒀭𒌓𒆠), which is found in the Persian court records at Persepolis from the reign of kings Darius I and Xerxes I. Several people in the court had this name, and the Persian records do not clearly identify any as having the same story and position as Mordecai. This name is considered evidence for the early composition of the Book of Esther, regardless of whether it was factual or fictional.

The Persian name Marduka was itself a transliteration of the Old Babylonian name ^{deity}Marduk (✳☐☐), which was the name of the Babylonian god called Bel in the Book of Daniel. The title Bel translates as Lord, however, the title was applied to many gods by the Babylonians. The most common god called Bel, was Marduk, the solar-calf god. The English name Mordecai is derived from the Hebrew name. The Mordecai in the book of Esther was said to have been born in Babylon, which would explain his having a Babylonian name. It is also evidence that the book likely originated in the early Persian era, as by the latePersian era, Ezra was already trying to purge the non-Judean elements from the country, including the Israelite priesthoods he did not like. By the late Persian era, no one would have written a fictional story about a Judean named after Marduk.

4 Codex Vaticanus: Mardochaeos ho tou Iaerou tou Semiou tou Cisaeou (ΜΑΡΔΟΧΑΙΟC Ο ΤΟΥ ΙΑΙΡΟΥ ΤΟΥ CΕΜΕΙΟΥ ΤΟΥ ΚΙCΑΙΟΥ). Translation: Mardochaeos the of Iaerou of Semiou of Cisaeou

• Septuagint manuscript 319: Mardochaeos ho tou Iaeiros tou Semiou tou Cisaeou (ΜΑΡΔοχΑΙοc ο του ΙΑδίβοc του Cóμδίου του Κισδίου). Translation: Mardochaeos the of Iaerou of Semiou of Cisaeou

• Aleppo Codex (chapter 2): mrdky bn yåyr bn šmôy bn qyš (מרדכי בן יאיר בן שמעי בן קיש). Translation: Mrdky the son of Yayr the son of Shmay the son of Qysh

• Leningrad Codex (chapter 2): maredochai ben ya'ir ben-shim'i ben-kish (מָרְדֳּכַי בֶּן יָאִיר בֶּן־שִׁמְעִי בֶּן־קִישׁ). Translation: Maredochai the son of Yaair the son of Shimai the son of Kish

• Codex Monacensis (VL 130): Mardocheus filius Iair filii Semei filii Esuus. Translation: Mardocheus son of Iair son of Semei son of Esuus

Mordecai's lineage is repeated verbatim in the second chapter of the Vaticanus and Alpha versions, where he is introduced again, suggesting that the Vaticanus and Alpha versions may have been partially synchronized with the Masoretic version at some point. As the Greek and Latin names are translations of Hebrew or Aramaic versions of the name, the Hebrew version is used in this translation.

5 Codex Vaticanus: Ioudaeos (ΙΟΥΔΑΙΟC). Translation: Judahite (or Judean)

• Alpha Texts (chapter 2): Ioudaeos (ιουΔΔιοc). Translation: Judahite (or Judean)

• Aleppo Codex (chapter 2): Yhwdy (יהודי). Translation: Judahite (or Jew, Jewish)

• Leningrad Codex (chapter 2): Yehudi (יְהוּדִי). Translation: Judahite (or Jew, Jewish)

• Codex Monacensis (chapter 3): Iudaeus. Translation: Judean (or Jew)

All four source texts mention that he was one of the exiles in Babylon, who Nebuchadnezzar had taken from Jerusalem, however, the Vaticanus and Masoretic versions also specify that he was a Judahite in this sentence when they detail his family history. This has to be something that was added later in Judean history, likely after the segregation of the Samaritans from the other Judahites by Ezra the scribe. As both the Vaticanus and Masoretic versions originate in Judea, either under Greek rule or later in the Hasmonean dynasty, this addition makes sense politically in the era. It does however imply that the two copies that originated in the Seleucid Dynasty, the Alpha and Vetus Latina versions, originated in a land where that segregation was not relevant, such as the Seleucid provinces of Babylonia or Persia. As there is no evidence that Mordecai ever visited Judea, it is not possible to interpret this term as meaning Judean, and so the term Judahite is used.

6 Codex Vaticanus: Sousoes tê poli (ϲΟΥϹΟΙϹΤΗΠΟΛΕ). Translation: Susa the city

• Septuagint manuscript 319: Sousoes tê poli (Ϲοⴆⲟⲟⲓⲥ ⲧⲗ πⴆλ𝟨). Translation: Susa the city

• Aleppo Codex: Šwšn hbyrh (שׁוּשַׁן הַבִּירָה). Translation: Susa the capital, Susa the citadel

- Leningrad Codex: Shushan habbirah (שׁוּשַׁן הַבִּירָה).

Translation: Susa the capital, Susa the citadel

- Codex Monacensis (VL 130): Susis Thebari

Susa was the ancient Elamite capital city, which was conquered by the Persian king Cyrus II in 540 BC. Under his heir Cambyses II, Susa became one of the four capitals of the Persian Empire. Under Darius I the city was expanded as the winter capital, while Persepolis to the east was the summer capital. This situation continued under Xerxes I, and for the rest of the Persian Empire. The city did not begin declining until after the conquest of Alexandria.

The variation found in the Vetus Latina is a Latin transliteration of the Greek Sousoes tê bari (Σούσοις τη βάρε) which means being 'Susa the capital,' and is itself proof that the Vetus Latina was translated from a Greek source. This is consistent with the Hebrew Shushan habbirah (שׁוּשַׁן הַבִּירָה), which also means Susa the Capital. This was Susa's status from Cambyses II's reign until the Macedonians conquered the Persian Empire. The use of the terms polei (πόλει) in both the Vaticanus and Alpha versions could also be interpreted as 'fortified capital,' but is ambiguous, and could simply mean town, as it is generally translated. The Acropolis in Athens was an example of the term polis specifically referring to the capital, in this case, the 'high town' above the city. The capital buildings in Alexandria were also called the Polis in the Ptolemy's Egypt. Therefore, the term Polis is translated as 'capital city' in this translation, as all four source texts indicate that was in the original text.

7 Codex Vaticanus: Nabouchodonosor (ΝΑΒΟΥΧΟΔΟΝΟϹΟρ). Translation: Nebuchadnezzar

• Septuagint manuscript 319: Nabouchodonosor (Νᾱμουχοδονοσοβ). Translation: Nebuchadnezzar

• Aleppo Codex: Nbwkdnṣr (נבוכדנצר). Translation: Nebuchadnezzar

• Leningrad Codex: Nevuchadnetzar (נְבוּכַדְנָאצַּר). Translation: Nebuchadnezzar

• Codex Monacensis (VL 130): Nabuchodonosor. Translation: Nebuchadnezzar

Nebuchadnezzar II was the king of Babylonia that conquered the kingdom of Judah in 587 BC, and according to both the Judahite and Babylonian records, took a large number of Judahites back to Babylonia as a subject people. These people were released from captivity 48 years later when King Cyrus II of Persia conquered the Babylonian Empire.

8 Codex Vaticanus: Iechoniou (ιεχΟΝΙΟΥ). Translation: Jeconiah

• Septuagint manuscript 319: Iechonios (ιϭχονϕᾱϲ). Translation: Jeconiah

• Aleppo Codex (in Chapter 2): Yknyh (יכניה). Translation: Jeconiah

• Leningrad Codex (in Chapter 2): Yechaneyah (יְכָנְיָה).
Translation: Jeconiah

• Codex Monacensis (VL 130): Iechoniam. Translation:
Jeconiah

According to the Babylonian Chronicles and several
Judahite books, King Jeconiah of Judah was taken captive by
Nebuchadnezzar in 598 BC, and Judah was thereafter ruled
by Jeconiah's uncle Zedekiah until Zedekiah's siding with
the Egyptians in 587 BC and the kingdom of Judah's
destruction. Jeconiah is also recorded in Neo-Babylonian
records as Ya'u-kīnu (𒅀𒌑𒆠𒉡) the king of Yahudu,
specifically in the Jehoiachin's Rations Tablets, dated to 592
BC.

9 Codex Vaticanus: dracontes (ΔΡΑΚΟΝΤΕC). Translation:
dragons (or monsters, beasts)

• Septuagint manuscript 319: dracontes (δβαγλιοντός).
Translation: dragons (or monsters, beasts)

• Masoretic Text: section missing

• Codex Monacensis (VL 130): dracones. Translation:
dragons, snakes, serpents

10 Codex Vaticanus: dicaiôn ethnos (ΔΙΚΑΙωΝ ΕΘΝΟC).
Translation: lawful (legal) people (tribe, family, country,
nation)

- Septuagint manuscript 319: term missing

- Masoretic Text: section missing

- Codex Monacensis (VL 130): term missing

Only the Vaticanus version of Esther specifies that the dragons wanted people to attack the 'lawful people,' which at the time the book was set would have been all Israelites. However, the translator has previously specified that Mordecai was a Judahite, and this phrase was likely added by the translator as well, as he is implying the Judeans in this verse. The issue of the Judeans not being able to follow the laws found in the Torah was the central reason for the rebellion against the rule of the Seleucid Empire, which started in 165 BC. The final paragraph of the Vaticanus version of Esther states it was translated in Jerusalem, and given to Ptolemy and Cleopatra in the fourth year of their reign, and as these were most likely Cleopatra I Syra of the Seleucid Empire and her husband Ptolemy V of Egypt, the book would have been given to them in the year 181 BC.

This addition of the term 'lawful people' against which the two mighty dragons were raising armies, could be interpreted as a warning to Ptolemy and Cleopatra to not stop the Judeans from following the law, which would explain why the translator created this version and gave it to the monarchs. Nevertheless, the dream itself, which is missing from the later Hebrew translation, is found in the Alpha and Vetus Latina versions of Esther, both of which appear to have been translated elsewhere in the Seleucid Empire, and likely earlier than the others.

11 Codex Vaticanus: theon (ⲐⲈⲞⲚ). Translation: god

• Septuagint manuscript 319: Cyrios (Ⲕⲱⲣⲓⲟⲥ). Translation: lord

• Masoretic Text: section missing.

• Codex Monacensis (chapter 2): deus. Translation: god

The words for god, El (אֵל) and Elohim (אֱלֹהִים), and lord, Adoni (אֲדוֹנִי) and Baal (בַּעַל) are not mentioned in the Masoretic version of Esther, the Hebrew version is entirely non-religious. In the other three texts the terms god (θεόν / deus) and lord (κύριος / dominus) are used interchangeably. The Vaticanus and Vetus Latina versions of Esther also contains the term Lord the god (Κύριε ο θεὸς / Dominus deus) in more than one location. The Vetus Latina also uses the terms Highest Lord (Excelsis Dominus) and Highest God (Excelsis Deo). All these terms are translations of Aramaic and Persian terms, yet missing from the Masoretic version, implying that version was seriously altered when it was translated into Hebrew.

12 Codex Vaticanus: phôs (ⲫⲱⲥ). Translation: light

• Septuagint manuscript 319: phôs (ⲫⲟⲟⲥ). Translation: light

• Masoretic Text: section missing.

• Codex Monacensis (VL 130): lux (lux). Translation: light

This reference to the light and the sun rising is a reference to the light that rises before and sets after the sun each day. In ancient times, when the world was believed to be flat, the fact that the sky lightened before the sun broke over the horizon was viewed as proof that there was a sphere of light around the sun. This is now known to be caused by light hitting the upper atmosphere before the lower atmosphere, and the shape of the earth making it resemble a sphere.

The Greeks typically called this light the Eos ('Εως), while the Romans called this light Aurora, and the Canaanites had called this light Shahar (𐤔𐤇𐤓), all of which mean 'dawn,' however, all the existing translations do not call it dawn, but simply specify light. This implies a Zoroastrian influence on the author, which would place the original composition during the Persian era.

13 Codex Vaticanus: hêlios (ΗΛΙΟC). Translation: sun, Helios (Greek titan of the sun)

• Septuagint manuscript 319: Hêlios (Ηλιoc). Translation: sun, Helios (Greek titan of the sun)

• Masoretic Text: section missing.

• Codex Monacensis (VL 130): sol. Translation: sun, Sol (Latin god of the sun)

14 Codex Vaticanus: Gabatha (ΓΑΒΑΘΑ)

• Septuagint manuscript 319: Astaos (φοτλοc)

• Aleppo Codex (in Chapter 2): Bgtn (בגתן)

- Leningrad Codex (Chapter 2): Bigtān (בִּגְתָן)

- Vetus Latina (Chapter 2): Bartageus

The name's language of origin and meaning are unclear, however, it may be Sanskrit. The difficulty figuring out the language and meaning of the name is compounded by the fact that the source texts use different transliterations of the original name. Given the diversity of names in the sources, the name Gabatha is transliterated directly in this translation from the Vaticanus version.

15 Codex Vaticanus: Tharrha (ΘΑΡΡΑ)

- Septuagint manuscript 319: Thedeutes (Θεδευτες)

- Aleppo Codex (in Chapter 2): Trš (תרש)

- Leningrad Codex (Chapter 2): Teresh (תֶּרֶשׁ)

- Vetus Latina (Chapter 2): Thedestes

Unlike the first eunuch's name, this one is fairly similar in the source texts, and is believed to be derived from the Old Persian for 'desire.' Given that most scholars agree on the language and meaning of the name, the common translation of Teresh is used in this translation.

16 Codex Vaticanus: eunouchôn (ЄΥΝΟΥΧѠΝ). Translation: eunuchs

• Septuagint manuscript 319: eunouchôn (ѕυνοѣχοοɴ). Translation: eunuchs

• Aleppo Codex (in Chapter 2): srysy (סריסי). Translation: eunuch (or castrated, neuter)

• Leningrad Codex (Chapter 2): sarisei (סָרִיסֵי). Translation: eunuch (or castrated, neuter)

• Vetus Latina (Chapter 2): eunuchus. Translation: eunuch (or castrated man)

All of the sources use terms meaning 'eunuchs,' however, this is likely a Persian era mistranslation, when the Aramaic term srys (𐤑𐤓𐤎) was used as the translation for the Neo-Babylonian term ša rēši (𒇻𒊕), meaning eunuch, vizier, noble, gentleman or homosexual. This suggests the existence of a Neo-Babylonian precursor to the Aramaic book of Esther.

17 As this event would date to 484 BC if the king was Xerxes I, the events are likely related to revolts in Babylonia that year. In the summer 484 BC, two Babylonians led revolts against Persian rule. Shamash-eriba was recognized as king in the city of Sippar, in northern Babylonia, and within weeks Bel-shimanni was recognized as king in the towns of Borsippa and Dilbat in southern Babylonia. Bel-shimanni's revolt only lasted a few weeks, however, Shamash-eriba's revolt wasn't crushed until the following spring. As the assassination plot of the two eunuchs must have been related to either another monarch seizing the throne, or a rebellion within the empire, this timing does correlate with what was happening in the Persian Empire in Xerxes I's second year.

18 Codex Vaticanus: Aman (ᴀᴍᴀɴ)

- Septuagint manuscript 319: Aman (Ἀμὰν)

- Aleppo Codex (in Chapter 3): Hmn (המן)

- Leningrad Codex (Chapter 3): Haman (הָמָן)

- Vetus Latina (Chapter 3): Aman

This name is believed to be a transliteration of the Persian name Imanish (𐎡𐎶𐎴𐎡𐏁), which shows up in ancient Persian records from the era, as well as Greek records from the era as Omanus ('Ομανυς). As the Hebrew-derived name Haman is the most common, and the Greek and Latin variants are virtually identical, the common name Haman is used in this translation.

If this was the son of King Amyntas I of Macedonia, his father was dead before the story began, and his brother Alexander I was the hyparchos of Achaemenid Macedonia in year 2 of Xerxes I. In year 7, when Haman is elevated above everyone else in the court, 479 BC, the Persians lost control of the Greek mainland, and Alexander I became their most important ally in Greece. If the king of the story was Xerxes I's son Artaxerxes I, then Alexander I was still the king of Macedonia for the first 11 years of Artaxerxes reign, however, was no longer an ally of the Persians after the Greeks captured the fortified Persian port town of Eion, in southern Macedonia, in 474 BC. There is no way to correlate the reference to a Macedonian prince in the Persian court in the era of Artaxerxes III, nor was Aigai the capital of Macedonia after 399 BC, so the reference to it would have been anachronistic. In the letter in chapter 8, the king refers to Haman as being like a father to him, which confirms that Haman was older than the king.

19 Codex Vaticanus: Amadathou (ᴀᴍᴀᴅᴀⵔⵢ)

• Septuagint manuscript 319: Amadathou (Ἀμαδάθου)

• Aleppo Codex (in Chapter 3): hmdtå (המדתא)

• Leningrad Codex (Chapter 3): Hammedata(הַמְּדָתָא)

• Vetus Latina (Chapter 8): Medadatum

This appears to be a reference to King Amyntas I (Ἀμύντας), the vassal king of Achaemenid Macedonia under 512 to 498 BC. When he died, his son Alexander I became the hyparchos of Achaemenid Macedonia, after the full independence of Macedonia in 479 BC, became its king. This person, Amyntas, is also recorded as being a Macedonas (Μακεδόνας), and a Agagai (אֲגָגִי), in the various versions of Esther, both of which point to his being a Macedonian. The capital of Achaemenid Macedonia was the town of Aigae (Αἰγαὶ). This is clearly the interpretation that the translator of the Alpha version made when he interpreted Agagai as Macedonian.

Amyntas I died before the story began regardless of who the king was, however, if it was King Xerxes I, the reference to Haman being elevated above everyone else in year 7 makes sense because in Xerxes I's seventh regal year the Persians lost control of the Greek mainland, and Amyntas I's son Alexander I of Macedon became the Persians most important ally on the Greek mainland, and so his brother would have been important at the Persian court. Alexander I was still the king of Macedonia under Xerxes I's heir Artaxerxes I, however, was no longer an ally of Persia, and so it seems unlikely his brother would have had much influence under Artaxerxes I. There is no way to correlate the reference to a Macedonian prince in the Persian court in the era of Artaxerxes III, nor was Aigai the capital of Macedonia after 399 BC, so the reference to it would have been anachronistic.

The Latin name Medadatum appears to be a corruption of the Hebrew name Hammedata (הַמְּדָתָא) found earlier in Masoretic Esther.

It seems the Aramaic spelling of the Macedonian name and relative obscurity of the Macedonian's king resulted in the Greek and Hebrew translators not recognizing it and simply transliterating the name. This is not unexpected given that even Xerxes' name was no longer recognized, and the Macedonian pronunciation of the name is still lost today, nevertheless, the references are clear that this was King Amyntas I, and so his name is restored.

20 Codex Vaticanus: Bougaeos (ⲃⲟⲩⲅⲁⲓⲟⲥ)

• Septuagint manuscript 319: Macedôn (ⲙⲁⲗⲅⲁⲇ̄ⲛ).

Translation: Macedonian

• Aleppo Codex (in Chapter 3): Åggy (אַגָּגִי)

• Leningrad Codex (Chapter 3): Agagai (אֲגָגִי)

• Codex Monacensis (VL 130): name not included in the text

The meaning of the word Bougaeos (Βουγαιος) in Vaticanus version, as well as in chapter 8 of the Alpha version where it is used in the same way it is here in the Vaticanus version, is an unknown term, however, sometimes translated as bully or braggart. As it is used as a substitute for Macedonian in both places, it is likely an attempt to transliterate Brygoe (Βρύγοι) back into Greek from Aramaic. The Brygoe, more commonly called the Bryges in English, were a tribe of people that settled in Macedonia, northern Greece, and Albania shortly before the Persians invaded Greece

The term used in the Masoretic version is generally accepted as the name of a tribe, and is often assumed to be descended from the ancient Amalekite king Agag from the time of King Saul. An alternate theory is that Agagai (אֲגָגִי) is a reference to Aigae (Αἰγαί), the capital of Macedonia before 399 BC. This was clearly the way the translators of the Alpha version interpreted the word, resulting in the term Macedonians.

The translators of both the Vaticanus and Vetus Latina versions also later referred to Haman as being a Macedonian, and all three sources other than the Masoretic versions include a letter that refers to Haman as involved in a Macedonian plot to destabilize the Persian Empire. Clearly, the translator of the Vaticanus version did not want to offend the monarchs he was preparing the translation for, and so transliterated the word Bougaeos instead of translating it in this section of text where the Macedonian was being praised. It is worth noting that early in his reign, Ptolemy V had fought a major war against the Macedonians, and lost. Mentioning them in the book the translator was preparing for Ptolemy V and Cleopatra I would have not been well received, which would explain why he transliterated the word instead of translating it as Macedonian.

As the term is most likely originated in the name of the Bryge tribe, who lived in Macedonia and the southern Balkans, that name is restored in this translation.

21 Codex Vaticanus: Indicês (ɪΝѴιΚΗϹ). Translation: Indian

• Septuagint manuscript 319: Indicês cae Aithiopias (ɪΝѴιιιλσ ιλι Ѵιθιοπϕλϲ). Translation: Indian and Aethiopian

• Aleppo Codex: hdw wôd kwš (הדו ועד כוש). Translation: Indus and up to Kush

• Leningrad Codex: hoddu ve'ad-kush (הֹדּוּ וְעַד־כּוּשׁ).
Translation: Indus and up to Kush

• Codex Monacensis (VL 130): India usque Aethiopiam.
Translation: India and Aethiopia

All four source texts list India (or the Sindhu River) as one end of the Persian Empire, however, only three source texts list Kush (Aethiopia) at the other end. The Vaticanus version is the one version that does not mention Aethiopia in this section of text, and instead simply says "from India." It is later mentioned in the letter in chapter 8. The omission of Kush from the opening chapter of the Vaticanus translation was likely intentional. It is known that Ptolemy V, who was likely the Ptolemy the Vaticanus version was translated for, disliked the Kushites.

It is believed that they became involved in the dynastic struggles in Egypt during Ptolemy IV, which caused Ptolemy V to dislike them, however, the exact events are unknown today. Nevertheless, if this translator in Jerusalem wanted King Ptolemy V to read his work, he would not have mentioned the Kushites. After Ptolemy VI briefly occupied the Nubian lands in between Egypt and Kush, there is little evidence of the later Ptolemys having any contact with Kush, which supports Ptolemy V and Cleopatra I being the Ptolemy and Cleopatra mentioned in the postscript, and the year of translation as 181 BC.

It is also worth noting that the number of 127 lands is consistent across the source texts, although it is not clear what this relates to exactly. The empire was divided into 36 satrapies (provinces) by Darius I, however, the satrapies were also subdivided into smaller districts, and it is not known how many of those there were. This is generally assumed to be a reference to those districts.

22 Codex Vaticanus: tritô eti (ΤΡΙΤѠЄΤЄ). Translation: third year

• Septuagint manuscript 319: year not mentioned

• Aleppo Codex: šnt šlwš (שׁנת שׁלושׁ). Translation: year three

• Leningrad Codex: shenat shalovosh (שְׁנַת שָׁלוֹשׁ). Translation: year three

• Codex Monacensis (VL 130): duodecimo anno. Translation: twelfth year

The Vaticanus and Masoretic versions, which both appear to be younger translations done in Judea, agree that this was the King's third year, however, the Vetus Latin version claimed it was his twelfth year, and the Alpha version does not mention a year. The difference between Xerxes I's third and twelfth years is significant. In 483 BC, Xerxes began planing his invasion of Greece, and did call in the satraps (governors) from across the empire to plan the offensive.

Two bridges were built across the Hellespont to allow for easy troop movements from Anatolia to the Balkans, the Xerxes Canal was dug through the isthmus of the Mount

Athos peninsula, and a vast army from across the empire was raised, including Achaean Greeks, Aegean Greeks, Aeolian Greeks, Assyrians, Babylonians, Black Sea Greeks, Colchians, Egyptians, Indians, Ionian Greeks, Judeans, Macedonians, Paeonians, Phoenicians, and Thracians. It took around three years for the invasion force to be mobilized, and they set out in 480 BC. Therefore, the description of Xerxes I calling his satraps to the capital in 483 BC makes sense.

The war was short, and Xerxes negotiated a treaty with the Greeks, following which he did not launch any major wars, and instead focused on construction projects, including the Palace of Darius in Susa, which is likely where most of this story was set. Susa was reported to be the favorite capital of Darius I, which was why he built the Palace. Xerxes then greatly expanded it after returning from Greece. Later Persian kings also expanded the Palace, including Artaxerxes I, Darius II, and Artaxerxes II. In Xerxes I's twelfth year, which is mentioned somewhere in all versions of Esther, nothing significant is recorded as happening that would require all the satraps to visit the capital, however, the Vetus Latina does not mention the satraps being present.

For comparison, when Artaxerxes I assumed the throne, in 465 BC, Egypt revolted, and he was not able to restore control until 454 BC, his eleventh year. It is therefore entirely plausible that he would have held a celebration in his twelfth year, when the empire was at peace for the first time in over a decade.

Meanwhile, in Artaxerxes III's second year, 356 BC, he attempted to dismiss Artabazus II from his satrapy of Hellespontine Phrygia, Artabazus started a rebellion that did not end until 354 BC, Artaxerxes III's fourth year, and it is very unlikely that he would have called the satraps to the capital during a rebellion of a satrap. At that point, the last thing he would want is all the satraps in the same place where they could conspire against him. His twelfth year would have been 346 BC, which would have been during the rebellion of the satraps of Sidon and Cyprus, again, not a time when he would have invited all the satraps to the same location, however, the Vetus Latina does not include them being present. Nevertheless, the chronology of the king in Esther does not correlate with the life of Artaxerxes III.

23 Codex Vaticanus: satrapôn (ϲατραπων). Translation: satrapies (provinces)

• Septuagint manuscript 319: chôres (χωρας). Translation: lands

• Aleppo Codex: mdynwt (מדינות). Translation: countries, lands, provinces, regions

• Leningrad Codex: medinovt (מְדִינֹות). Translation: countries, lands, provinces, regions

• Codex Monacensis (VL 130): does not mention the governors of the empire being invited, just those in Susa Thebari

It is unclear why the Vetus Latina deviates so much here, as it both have the deviation of "twelfth year," instead of "third year," and does not mention the satraps being present. The other three source texts mention the governors of the satrapies being present, and the Vaticanus version even maintains the Persian name, which does support its authenticity on this issue.

24 Codex Vaticanus: Parinou (ΠΑΡΙΝΟΥ). Translation: Parian

- Septuagint manuscript 319: Parinou (ΠΑΡϚ̑νου).

Translation: Parian

- Aleppo Codex: ômwdy (עְמוּדי). Translation: pillar

- Leningrad Codex: ammudei (עַמּוּדֵי). Translation: pillar

- Codex Monacensis (VL 130): Paros. Translation: Paros

Parian Marble was from the Island of Paros in the Aegean Sea. It was highly prized by the Greeks, and many ancient statues were carved in it, including the Winged Victory of Samothrace. The mines of Paros were in use since at least the 6th century BC.

25 Codex Vaticanus: Astin (ΑϹΤΙΝ)

- Septuagint manuscript 319: Ouastin (Ουάστιν)

- Aleppo Codex: Wšty (וַשְׁתִּי)

- Leningrad Codex: Vashti (וַשְׁתִּי)
- Codex Monacensis (VL 130): Vasthi

If the king in Esther was Xerxes I, then this queen would have most likely been Amāstrī (𐎠𐎶𐎿𐎫𐎼), known in Greek records from the era as Amestris (Ἄμηστρις), Ámāstris (Ἄμαστρις), or Amastrinē (Ἀμαστρινε). Xerxes I was already married to Amastri before Darius I died. It had been a political wedding, as her father Otanes had been one of the seven Persians that helped Xerxes I kill his predecessor King Bardiya (or a magical doppelganger named Gaumata) and seize the Persian throne. She lived a long time, and is believed to have died in 424 BC, probably at more than 80 years old. The ancient Greeks accused her of making human sacrifices to Hades in order to live so long, however, there is no evidence of human sacrifice in the Persian Empire, and Persian law expressly forbade it.

Conversely, if this was the queen of King Artaxerxes I, it would have been Queen Damaspia. While Artaxerxes I did take additional wives, he appears to have remained close to Damaspia until they both died in 424 BC, while traveling together. If this was Artaxerxes III, then it was probably Atossa, however, little is known about their relationship.

As this story appears to be about Xerxes I, whose name was forgotten by the time of the various translations were made, it is understandable that the name of his wife was also no longer understood by the time the translations were made.

26 Codex Vaticanus: Aman cae Bazan cae Tharrha cae Bôrazê cae Zatholtha cae Abataza cae Tharaba (ΑΜΑΝ ΚΑΙ ΒΑΖΑΝ ΚΑΙ ΘΑΡΡΑ ΚΑΙ ΒѠΡΑΖΗ ΚΑΙ ΖΑΘΟΛΘΑ ΚΑΙ ΑΒΑΤΑΖΑ ΚΑΙ ΘΑΡΑΒΑ). Translation: Aman and Bazan and Tharrha and Bôrazê and Zatholtha and Abataza and Tharaba

• Septuagint manuscript 319: the names are not mentioned in the verse

• Aleppo Codex: mhwmn bztå hrbwnå bgtå wåbgtå ztr wkrks (מהומן בזתא חרבונא בגתא ואבגתא זתר וכרכס). Translation: Mhwmn, Bztå, Ḥrbwnå, Bgtå, Wåbgtå, Ztr, and Krks

• Leningrad Codex: mehuman bizzeta charvovna bigta va'avagta zetar vecharkas (מְהוּמָן בִּזְּתָא חַרְבוֹנָא בִּגְתָא וַאֲבַגְתָא זֵתַר וְכַרְכַּס). General translation: Mehuman, Bizzeta, Charvovna, Bigta, and Avagta, Zetar, and Charkas

• Codex Monacensis (VL 130): Maosma et Narbona et Nabattha et Zatai et Achedes et Thares et Tarecta. Translation: Maosma and Narbona and Nabattha and Zatai and Achedes and Thares and Tarecta

The three source texts that include the names do not use the same set of names. The first name in the Vaticanus version is Aman, the same name as used previously in the chapter for Aman Amadathou (Haman ben Hammedatha), which suggests that this is the same person, however, the names are not the same in the Masoretic or Vetus Latina versions, where Mehuman and Maosma are used respectively.

The Vaticanus version also includes the name Tharra (Θαρρα), which is one of the names of the eunuchs that plotted against the king the year before. The name of eunuch that was killed was Teresh (תֶּרֶשׁ) and Thedestes in the Masoretic and Vetus Latina versions of Esther, however, the equivalent name in this list of the Vaticanus version's Tharrha is Charvovna (חַרְבוֹנָא) and Nabattha. The Masoretic version also includes the name Bigta (בִּגְתָא) which some scholars believe is an alternate for of Bigtan (בִּגְתָן), the other eunuch that was plotting to kill the king. The equivalent names are Bôrazê (Βωραζη) and Zatai in this list, however, the plotting eunuch's names were Gabatha (Γαβαθα) and Bartageus in the Vaticanus and Vetus Latina versions. As none of these sets of names confirm the others, the names are transliterated directly from the Vaticanus Codex in this translation.

27 Codex Vaticanus: Arcesaeos cae Sarsathaeos cae Malêsear (ΑΡΚΕϹΑΙΟϹ ΚΑΙ ϹΑΡϹΑΘΑΙΟϹ ΚΑΙ ΜΑΛΗϹΕΑΡ). Translation: Arcesaeos and Sarsathaeos and Malêsear

• Septuagint manuscript 319: the names are not mentioned in the verse

• Aleppo Codex: kršnå štr ådmtå tršyš mrs mrsnå mmwkn (כרשנא שתר אדמתא תרשיש מרס מרסנא ממוכן). Translation: Kršnå Štr ådmtå Tršyš Mrs Mrsnå Mmwkn

• Leningrad Codex: karshena shetar admata tarshish meres marsena memuchan (כַּרְשְׁנָא שֵׁתָר אַדְמָתָא תַרְשִׁישׁ מֶרֶס מַרְסְנָא)

מְמוּכָן). General translation: Karshena, Shetar, Admata, Tarshish, Meres, Marsena, Memuchan

• Codex Monacensis (VL 130): Mordecai et Sorathaeas et Pabataleus et Malesath et Mucheas. Translation: Mordecai and Sorathaeas and Pabataleus and Malesath and Mucheas

All three of the source texts that maintain a list of names for the Persian and Median officials have a different number of officials, however, some of the names do seem to have a common origin. The Vaticanus' Sarsathaeos (Σαρσαθαιος), and Vetus Latina's Sorathaeas, are the same name, and indicating this name was likely in the Aramaic source text. The Masoretic name Shetar (שֵׁתָר) may be derived from the same name, however, the Hebrew name appears to be derived from the Avestan name Tishtrya.

Tishtrya was a rain and fertility deity/being in the Avesta, the Zoroastrian holy book. The Vaticanus name Malêsear (Μαλησεαρ), may share a common origin with the Vetus Latina's Malesath, however, neither close to any of the names found in the Masoretic Text. Mordecai is only mentioned in the Vetus Latina, and seems improbable that Mordecai was a Persian or Median official given the rest of the story. As none of the lists confirm each other, the Vaticanus list is transliterated in this translation.

28 Codex Vaticanus: Mouchaeos (ΜΟΥΧΑΙΟC)

• Septuagint manuscript 319: Bougaeos (Βουγαιος)

• Aleppo Codex: mwmkn [mmwkn] (מומכן [ממוכן])

• Leningrad Codex: mumechan K [memuchan Q] (ב מומכן
[ק ממוכן])

• Codex Monacensis (VL 130): Mordecai

None of the names is a close match, and again, as in the previous name list, Modecai is present in the Vetus Latina, but not the other source texts. The Masoretic name Mumechan / Memuchan (מומכן / ממוכן) is identical to the name Memuchan (ממוכן) from the previous name list of Persian and Median officials, other than the different vowel points and accents added by the Masorites to the K variant, and this is probably intended to represent the same person. The Vaticanus' name Mouchaeos (Μουχαιος) appears from nowhere, and may be an attempt to transliterate the name Memuchan (ממוכן) into Greek. If so, Mouchaeos may have once been part of the list of three officials found in the Vaticanus' version, however, it is equally possible that the translation of the Masoretic version simply added Memuchon to the previous list of officials in order to clarify who this person was, and why they were suddenly talking to the king.

The Alpha version's Bougaeos (Βουγαιος) appears from nowhere but is less conspicuous as the Alpha version did not include a list of who the king was talking to. The name

Bougaeos is also unrelated to the various names in all three of the previous lists of officials. The term Bougaeos appears to be derived from an Aramaic translation of Bryges (Βρύγοι), as the word is used interchangeably with Macedonian (Μακεδών), which suggests that Haman is the one who made the suggestion.

The Vetus Latina inclusion of Mordecai again, and having him make the suggestion to the king to punish the Queen seems out of place in the overall narrative of the story, as does him being one of the Persian and Median officials. It seems the intent of the translator of the Vetus Latina version of Esther was to elevate Mordecai, who in Rabbinical Judaism is considered less important than Esther in the book of Esther. As the names don't correlate, the name Mouchaeos is transliterated directly from the Codex Vaticanus in this translation.

Esther (Vaticanus): Chapter 2

After this, the king's anger was pacified, and he no longer thought of Astin, or remembered what she had said, and how he had condemned her. Then the servants of the king said, "Let there be found for the king chaste and beautiful young virgins. Let the king appoint local governors in all the provinces of his kingdom, and let them select beautiful and chaste young girls and bring them to the city of Susa, to the women's apartment, and let them be consigned to the king's eunuch, the keeper of the women, and let things for purification and other attendance be given to them. Let the woman who pleases the king become queen instead of Astin."

The idea pleased the king, and so he ordered it. There was a Judahite in the city of Susa, and his name was Mordecai the son of Jair the son of Shimei the son of Kish, of the tribe of Benjamin, who was a captive from Jerusalem, which had been captured by King Nebuchadnezzar of Babylon. He had a foster child, the daughter of Abinadab[1] his father's brother. Her name was Esther, and after her parents had died he raised her to be a wife for himself, as the girl was beautiful. Because the king's ordinance was published, many girls were gathered to the city of Susa under the hand of Hegai,[2] and Esther was brought to Hegai the keeper of the women.

The girl pleased him, and she found favor in his sight, and he rushed to give her the things for purification, and her portion and the seven girls appointed to her from the palace, and he treated her and her girls well in the women's apartment. But Esther didn't reveal her family or her families, for Mordecai had ordered her not to tell. Mordecai walked to the women's court every day to see what would become of Esther. It came time for a virgin to go into the king after she should have waited twelve months, for so are the days of purification fulfilled, six months while they are anointing themselves with oil of myrrh, and six months with spices and women's purification.

Then the girl went to the king, and the officer to whoever he will give the command would bring her in with him from the women's apartment to the king's chamber. She entered in the evening, and in the morning she departed to the second women's apartment, where Hegai the king's eunuch was the keeper of the women, and she did not go to the king again unless she was called by name. When the time was fulfilled for Esther to go to the king, she neglected nothing that the eunuch commanded, and Esther found grace in the sight of all that looked on her.

Esther went to King Artaxerxes in the twelfth month, which is Adar,[3] in the seventh year of his reign.[4]

The king loved Esther, and she found favor beyond all the other virgins, and he put on her the queen's diadem. The king made a banquet for all his friends and great men for seven days, and he celebrated his marriage to Esther, and he released from debt all those who were under his dominion.

Mordecai was serving in the palace, and until now Esther had not revealed her families, for Mordecai commanded her so, and to fear God, and follow his commandments, as when she was with him, and Esther did not change her way of living.

[Two eunuchs of the king, the chiefs of the body-guards, were angry because Mordecai was promoted, and they wanted to kill King Artaxerxes. The matter was revealed to Mordecai, and he made it known to Esther, and she told the king about the conspiracy. The king questioned the two eunuchs, and hanged them, and the king gave orders to make a record for a memorial in the royal records of the good offices of Mordecai, as a commendation.][5]

Esther (Vaticanus): Chapter 2 Notes

1 Codex Vaticanus: Aminadab (ᴀᴍɪɴᴀᴅᴀʙ)

- Septuagint manuscript 319: his name is not mentioned

- Masoretic Text: his name is not mentioned

- Vetus Latina (later in the chapter): Abihail

The Vetus Latina's Abihail is likely a scribal error, as in chapter 9 the father of Esther is called Aminadab.

2 Codex Vaticanus: Gai (ᴦᴀɪ)

- Septuagint manuscript 319: Gogaios (ᴦογᴅιος)

- Aleppo Codex: hgy (הגי)

- Leningrad Codex: hegai (הֵגַי)

- Codex Monacensis (VL 130): Hegai

As the four names are related, the Latin Hegai is used in this translation, as it is the most common English rendering of the name, and is similar to the Hebrew pronunciation.

3 Codex Vaticanus: Adar (ᴀᴅᴀρ)

- Septuagint manuscript 319: month not mentioned

- Aleppo Codex: ṭbt (טבת)

- Leningrad Codex: tevet (טֵבֵת)

- Codex Monacensis (VL 130): Adar

The month of Adar is the twelfth month of the Hebrew ecclesiastical calendar, and corresponds approximately to late February and early March on the Gregorian calendar. The month of Tevet is the tenth month of the Hebrew ecclesiastical calendar, and corresponds approximately to late December and early January on the Gregorian calendar. It is unclear why the texts contain this dependency, however, this translation follows the Vaticanus version and so uses the name Adar.

4 The Vaticanus, Masoretic, and Vetus Latina versions of Esther all agree that this was the king's seventh year, while the Alpha version does not specify a year. If this was King Xerxes I, then this would have been the year 479 BC. At the time Xerxes was still engaged in his major construction projects across the empire, including the expansions of the Palace of Darius in Susa, where the story is set.

If this was King Artaxerxes I, then this would have been in the year 458 BC, during Artaxerxes I's campaigns to reconquer Egypt, and defend his empire from rampaging hordes of Greek mercenaries. As he was probably not in Susa for several years during this time, it is very unlikely that this story was about him.

If this was Artaxerxes III, then this would have been the year 351 BC. This is the year that Artaxerxes III launched his first campaign to reconquer Egypt, and it was a complete failure, leading to the satraps across Anatolia, Cyprus, and Phoenicia declaring independence, and it is believed he did not return to Susa until sometime in 350 BC, meaning this story is almost certainly not about him.

5 This last section of chapter 2 is missing from the Alpha version, but found in the rest, essentially retelling the story from the Vaticanus, Alpha, and Vetus Latina versions chapter 1, which is missing from the Masoretic version. The Vetus Latina version even names the two eunuchs Bartageus and Thedestes, the same names as given in chapter 1. This event could not have taken place in both year 2 and year 7, and therefore this last section of chapter 2 (Masoretic chapter 1) must have been copied from a proto-Masoretic version of Esther at some point into the Vaticanus and Vetus Latina versions of Esther. The Alpha version appears to have been rare enough that no one bothered adding the conflicting paragraphs to it.

Esther (Vaticanus): Chapter 3

After this, King Artaxerxes highly honored Haman the son of Amyntas, the Bryge, and praised him and placed him above all his friends. Everyone in the palace bowed before him as the king had ordered it, but Mordecai would not bow before him. Those in the king's palace asked Mordecai, "Mordecai, why do you disobey the commands of the king?"

They spoke to him everyday, but he did not listen to them, so they told Haman that Mordecai resisted the commands of the king, and Mordecai had shown to them that he was a Judahite. When Haman understood that Mordecai did not bow before him, he was greatly enraged and made plans to completely destroy all the Judahites who were under the rule of Artaxerxes.

He made a decree in the twelfth[1] year of the reign of Artaxerxes, and cast lots for the day and month on which he would kill the people of Mordecai, and the lot fell on the fourteenth day of the month of Adar.[2] He told King Artaxerxes, "There is a nation scattered among the nations in all your kingdom, and their laws differ from those of all the other nations, and they disobey the laws of the king. It is not good for the king to leave them alone. If it seems good to the king, let him make a decree to destroy them, and I will deposit into the king's treasury ten thousand talents of silver."

The king took off his ring, and gave it into the hands of Haman, to seal the decrees against the Judahites, and the king said to Haman, "Keep the silver, but treat the nation as you want."

So the king's scribes were called in the first month, on the thirteenth day, and they recorded as Haman commanded the captains and governors in every province, from India all the way to Kush, to all 127 districts, and to the rulers of the nations according to their several languages, in the name of King Artaxerxes. The message was sent by posts throughout the kingdom of Artaxerxes, to destroy completely the people of the Judahites on the first day of the twelfth month, which is Adar, and to plunder their property. The following is a copy of the letter:

> The great king Artaxerxes writes this to the rulers and lesser satraps of 127 districts from India to Kush, who hold authority under him. Ruling over many nations and having obtained dominion over the whole world, I thought, not elated by the confidence of power, but ever conducting myself with great moderation and gentleness, to make the lives of my subjects continually tranquil, desiring both to maintain the kingdom quiet and orderly to its utmost limits, and to restore the peace desired by all men.

> But when I had inquired of my counselors how this should be brought to pass. Haman, who excels in soundness of judgment among us, and has been manifestly well in-

clined without wavering and with unshaken fidelity, and had obtained the second post in the kingdom, informed us that a certain ill-disposed people is mixed among all the tribes throughout the world, opposed in their law to every other nation, and continually neglecting the commands of the king, so that the united government blamelessly administered by us is not quietly established.

Having then conceived that this nation alone of all others is continually set in opposition to every man, introducing as a change a foreign code of laws, and evilly plotting to accomplish the worst injuries against our interests, and against the happy establishment of the monarchy, we signified to you in the letter written by Haman, who is set over the public affairs and is our second governor, to destroy them all completely with their wives and children by the swords of the enemies, without pitying or restraint, on the fourteenth day of the twelfth month Adar,[3] of the present year. The people previously and now ill-disposed to us having been violently consigned to Hades[4] in one day, may from now on secure to us continually a well-constituted and quiet state of affairs.

The copies of the letters were published in every province, and an order was given to all the nations to be ready against that day. The business was hastened, and that at Susa, and the king and Haman began to drink, but the city was troubled.

Esther (Vaticanus): Chapter 3 Notes

1 Codex Vaticanus: dôdecatô (ⲇⲱⲆⲈⲕⲀⲦⲱⲓ). Translation: twelfth

- Septuagint manuscript 319: year not mentioned

- Aleppo Codex: štym ôšrh (שתים עשרה). Translation: twelve

- Leningrad Codex: sheteim esreh (שְׁתֵּים עֶשְׂרֵה). Translation: twelve

- Codex Monacensis (VL 130): duodecimo. Translation: twelfth

If this was King Xerxes I, then this would have been the year 474 BC. At the time Xerxes was still engaged in his major construction projects across the empire, including the expansions of the Palace of Darius in Susa, where the story is set. If this was King Artaxerxes I, then this would have been in the year 453 BC, the year after Artaxerxes I reconquered Egypt.

2 Codex Vaticanus: Adar (ⲀⲆⲀⲣ)

- Septuagint manuscript 319: Adar Nisan (ⲀⲆⲁⲛⲃ Νιⲥⲁ)

- Aleppo Codex: Ådr (אדר). Translation: Adar

- Leningrad Codex: Adar (אֲדָר)

- Codex Monacensis (VL 130): Adar

The Alpha version is the only one of the four source texts that use the name Adar-Nisan, like in chapter 1, and again this year in Xerxes reign, 474 BC, was a leap year meaning there was a second month of Adar. Conversely, this year in Artaxerxes I's reign, 453 BC, was not a leap year, and so there was not a second month of Adar.

3 Codex Vaticanus: Adar (ᐱᐞᐱᵽ)

- Septuagint manuscript 319: Adar (ᐱᐞɑᴎᵽ)

- Masoretic Text: name not mentioned

- Codex Monacensis (VL 130): Adar

The Alpha version shows a difference between this reference to Adar, and the former reference to Adar-Nisan, implying that the letter that was being sent out throughout the empire was referring to the Adar twelve months after the Adar the letter was written in. This would make the month Adar, not Adar Bet, which seems to be what the Alpha version is recording. The Alpha version also records that Adar was Dystros (Δύστρος), the equivalent on the Macedonian calendar.

4 Codex Vaticanus: Aedên (αιδην). Translation: Hades (Greek god of the underworld), Hades (underworld), grave, death

- Septuagint manuscript 319: Hadên (ᐱιᐞᴌᴎ). Translation: Hades (Greek god of the underworld), Hades (underworld), grave, death

- Masoretic Text: name not mentioned

- Codex Monacensis (VL 130): Orcus. Translation: Translation: Orcus (Roman god of the underworld)

Esther (Vaticanus): Chapter 4

When Mordecai heard what was done, he tore his garments and put on sackcloth, and sprinkled dust on himself. He rushed out into the open street of the city, and cried with a loud voice, "A nation that has done no wrong is going to be destroyed!"

He came to the king's gate, and stood, for it was not legal for him to enter into the palace wearing sackcloth and ashes. In every district where the letters were posted, there was crying and lamentation and great mourning on the part of the Judahites. They covered themselves in sackcloth and ashes. The queen's maids and eunuchs went in and told her, and when she heard what was done, she was disturbed, and she sent a messenger to dress Mordecai, and take off his sackcloth, but he would not agree to it.

Esther called for her eunuch Hathach,[1] who waited on her, and she sent to learn the truth from Mordecai. Mordecai showed him what was done, and the promise which Haman had made the king of ten thousand talents to be paid into the treasury, so he might destroy the Judahites. He gave him a copy of the writing that was published in Susa concerning their destruction, to show to Esther, and told him to order her to go in and beg the king, and to plead from him for the people. "Remember," he said, "the days of your low beginning, and how you were nursed by my hand because Haman who holds the place next to the king has spoken against us for death. Visit the king and speak concerning us, to save us from death."

Hathach went in and told her all these words, and Esther said to Hathach, "Go to Mordecai and say, 'All the nations of the empire know, that whoever, man or woman, will go to the king in the inner court uncalled, that person can not live. Only whomever the king will stretch out his golden scepter to, will live, and I have not been called to go to the king for thirty days.'"

Hathach reported to Mordecai all the words of Esther. Then Mordecai said to Hathach, "Go and tell her, 'Esther, don't convince yourself that you alone will escape in all the kingdom, out of all the Judahites. For if you will refuse to listen on this occasion, help, and protection will come to the Judahites from another source, but you and your father's house will perish, and who knows, if you have been made queen for this very occasion?"

Esther sent the man that came to her back to Mordecai with the response, "Go and assemble the Judahites that are in Susa, and fast for me, and don't eat or drink for three days, both night and day, and I also with my girls will fast, and then I will go to the king contrary to the law, even if I must die."

Mordecai went and did all that Esther commanded him. He implored the Lord, making mention of all the works of the Lord, and he said, "Lord, Lord Moloch[2] ruling over all. All things are in your power, and there is no one who will oppose you, in your purpose to save Israel. You have made the sky and the land and every wonderful thing in the world under the sky. You are lord of all, and there is no one who will resist you, Lord. You know all things, you know, Lord, that it is not in insolence or haughtiness or love of glory, that I have done this, to refuse obeisance to the haughty Haman. I would gladly have kissed the soles of his feet for the safety of Israel. I have done this so I might not set the glory of man above the glory of God, and I will not worship anyone except you Lord, and I will not do these things in haughtiness. Now, Lord God Moloch,[3] the god of Abraham, spare your people, for our enemies are looking on us to our destruction, and they have desired to destroy your ancient inheritance. Do not overlook your people, who you have saved for yourself out of the land of Egypt. Listen to my prayer, and be propitious to your inheritance, and turn our mourning into gladness, that we may live and sing praise to your name, Lord, and do not completely destroy the mouth of those who praise you, Lord."

All Israel cried with all their might, for death was before their eyes. Queen Esther searched for herself a refuge in the Lord, being taken as it were in the agony of death. Having taken off her glorious apparel, she put on garments of distress and mourning, and instead of grand perfumes she filled her head with ashes and dung, and she greatly brought down her body, and she filled every place of her glad adorning with the torn curls of her hair.

She implored the Lord God of Israel, "Lord, you alone are our king, help me who am destitute, and have no helper but you, for my danger is near at hand. I have heard from my birth, in the tribe of my families that you, Lord, took Israel out of all the nations, and our fathers out of all their families for a perpetual inheritance, and have worked for them all that you have said. Now we have sinned before you, and you have delivered us into the hands of our enemies because we honored their gods."

"You are righteous, Lord. But now they have not been contented with the bitterness of our slavery, but have laid their hands on the hands of their idols, in order to abolish the decree of your mouth, and completely destroy your inheritance, and to stop the mouth of those who praise you, and to extinguish the glory of your temple and your altar, and to open the mouth of the nations to speak the praises of vanities, and in order that a mortal king should be admired forever. Lord, do not resign your scepter to them that are not, and let them not laugh at our fall, but turn their counsel against themselves and make an example of him who has begun to injure us. Remember us, Lord, manifest yourself in the time of our affliction and encourage me, king of gods,[4] and ruler of all dominion. Put harmonious speech into my mouth before the lion, and turn his heart to hate he who fights against us, to the utter destruction of he who consents with him. But deliver us by your hand, and help me who am destitute, and have none but the Lord."

"You know all things, and know that I hate the glory of transgressors and that I abhor the bed of the uncircumcised, and of every foreigner. You know my necessity, for I abhor the symbol of my proud station, which is on my head in the days of my splendor. I abhor it like a menstruation cloth, and I do not wear it on days when I am alone. Your handmaid has not eaten at the table of Haman, and I have not honored the banquet of the king, nor have I drunk wine of libations. Neither has your handmaid rejoiced since the day of my promotion until now, except in you, Lord God of Abraham. God, who has power over all, listen to the voice of the desperate, and deliver us from the hand of those that plan violence, and deliver me from my fear."

Esther (Vaticanus): Chapter 4 Notes

1 Codex Vaticanus: Achrathaeon (ΑΧΡΑΘΑΙΟΝ)

• Septuagint manuscript 319: name not mentioned

• Aleppo Codex: htk (חתך)

• Leningrad Codex: Hatach (הֲתָךְ)

• Codex Monacensis (VL 130): Hathach

As the three names appear to be related, and so the most common English variant Hathach is used.

2 Codex Vaticanus: Cyrie Cyrie Basileu (ΚΥΡΙΕΚΥΡΙΕ ΒΑCΙΛΕΥ). Translation: Lord Lord King

• Septuagint manuscript 319: Cyrie pantocratôr (Κᾱρΐϲ παντοιβαγντορβ). Translation: Lord Omnipotent (or Almighty)

• Masoretic Text: section missing

• Codex Monacensis (VL 130): deum Abraham et deum Isaac et deum Iacob. Translation: god of Abraham and god of Isaac and god of Jacob

The three source texts with names, use terms that are not direct translations of each other, however, two of them are directly related to the term šdy (ZΔW), which was generally transliterated as šadday (שַׁדַּי) in the Masoretic Text, and translated as Omnipotent (παντοκράτωρ) in the Septuagint. Shadday was the term used to describe the god of Abraham, Isaac, and Jacob in the Masoretic text, suggesting that the Alpha Texts and Vetus Latin versions have a common origin. Nevertheless, based on the general content of the various forms of Esther, and the fact that the name was redacted from the Masoretic translation, it seems apparent that Vaticanus version includes a translation original name.

The Septuagint and Masoretic translations often differ in regards to the name or title Shadday, suggesting that the Aramaic and Canaanite (Judahite or Samaritan) source texts they worked from differed in regards to this word. The term was omitted throughout the Septuagint's Cosmic Genesis, Exodus, and Numbers, however, was the name of the god of Abraham, Isaac, Jacob, and Moses in Masoretic Bereshít, Exodus, and Numbers. It is used consistently in Masoretic Bereshít and Numbers, and is mentioned again in Masoretic Exodus when Moses god's name Ôn (Ωv) is introduced in the Septuagint's Exodus. As the name was most likely the name that King Manasseh cut out of the Aramaic translation of the Torah, he was probably the one who substituted the name Ôn (Ωv).

In the book of Hosea, which was set in Samaria in decades before it was conquered by the Assyrians, Hosea warned the Samaritans not to worship a god named Ôn (Ωv) / Aven (אָוֶן). Hosea lived during the decline of the Kingdom of Samaria, and disappeared during the three year Assyrian war against Samaria, which ended in the destruction of Samaria in 722 BC. The earliest Aramaic translation of the Torah, appears to have been a translation of Cosmic Genesis, Exodus, and Numbers made during the life of King Hezekiah, specifically between the years 715 and 706 BC, based on the references in the genealogy of nations, and the mention of Nineveh as the capital.

The Greek Ôn (Ωυ) and Hebrew Aven (אֶוֶן), are both almost certainly derived from the name Ān (ᛁ), the Neo-Assyrian name of the original Sumerian sky-father [deity]Ān (𒀭𒀭). The word was generally known as Ilu (𒀭) in Eastern Semitic languages, and spelled as Ỉl (𒂊𒐖) in Ugaritic, Ảl (𐤀𐤋) in Phoenician, Ảlhå (אלהא) in Aramaic, and El (אֵל) in Hebrew. The alternate pronunciation of Ān was used in Neo-Assyrian mythology to refer to [deity]Ān (ᛁᛁ), who was viewed as being the father of Aššur (ᛁ𒀸), the national god of the Assyrian Empire. This indicates that the Samaritans in Hosea's time had reinterpreted Shadday as Ān, and King Manasseh of Judah had added Åwn (און) to the Aramaic version of the Torah after he cut out Shadday's name.

The cause of the confusion over the term Shadday, is likely due to the difference between the meaning of the word in Canaanite versus Aramaic. In Akkadian cuneiform, which was adopted as the written script by many cultures, the term was [deity]šēdu (𒀭𒁲), however, it referred to a 'protective spirit' or 'lesser god.' In the later Aramaic language, the word became šydå (שידא), meaning 'demon' in the classical sense, as a type of muse or nymph. Whereas in Canaanite, šdy (𐤔𐤃𐤉) took on a different meaning, generally interpreted as 'powerful' by the Early Classical Era, which is likely where the Greeks ultimately derived the term 'omnipotent' (παντοκράτορος), which was used later in the Septuagint where the Masoretic Text generally uses the term šdy.

This alternate interpretation of the šdy (𐤔𐤃𐤉) in Canaanite is likely due to the Egyptian New Kingdom era rule over Canaan, when Shed (𓆓𓂻𓏛, transliteration: šd), was worshiped in the region. Shed, who was often referred to as 'the savior,' was virtually identical to the Hurrian god Aplu (𒀀𒉿), generally accepted as a shortened version of aplu ^iluEllil (𒀀𒉿 𒀭𒂗𒆤), an epithet of Marduk, the son of the Old Babylonian god Ellil. Both Shed and Ablu began post-Hyksos era as similar gods to the Amorite Resheph, a god of disease and destruction, and developed into gods of healing.

Ablu was also imported to the Neshite (Hittite) and Trojan civilizations as the god Apaliunas (𒀀𒉺𒇷𒌋𒈾𒀸), who was mentioned in a peace treaty between the civilizations in 1280 BC. Homer reported in the Illiad that Apollôn (Απολλων) was the god that built the wall of Troy, which confirms that the Greeks did view Apaliunas as Apollo. In the Illiad, a priest of Apollo called Chryses, referred to Apollo as the 'Lord of Mice' as he was believed to protect from plagues of mice. This suggests that the Pelesets viewed Shadday as a version of Apollo when they captured the box of the covenant in 1st Kingdoms (Masoretic Samuel), as they returned it with golden statues of mice after their cities were plagued by swarms of mice.

Ablu was Hurrian the name of Resheph under the rule of the Amorites, and Shed emerged as the replacement of Resheph in Southern Canaan during the New Kingdom era, after Resheph was largely suppressed in the aftermath of the fall of the Hyksos dynasty. In the Masoretic Book of Job, Eliphaz referred to humanity as the 'sons of Resheph' (בני-רשף) instead of the 'sons of Adam,' and then uses Shadday as the name of his god. This god Shadday was explicitly listed alongside the god El in Masoretic Job, whereas in the Septuagint's Job they are not explicitly listed as two separate gods. The Greek translation of Šdy (שדי) in Job is consistent with most of the Septuagint, using a term that translates as 'omnipotent' (παντοκράτορος), however, the name El (אל) is generally translated as a word meaning 'strong' (ἰσχυρὸς). The Masoretic text lists them side by side, as 'god El and god Šdy,' (אל-אל ואל-שדי), which the Greek translators did not do, instead routinely dropping the second reference to a god when they were listed together.

The terms 'god Šdy' (אל-שדי) and 'god El' (אל-אל) are repeatedly found in the Masoretic version of Job, and are themselves direct translations of the same terms in cuneiform: deityšēdu (✳⊞) and deityĀn (✳✳). Unfortunately, the Akkadian meaning of the word šēdu was 'demonic,' which is likely the cause of its redaction. Based on the linguistics of Masoretic Job, the text of the book existed in either hieratic Canaanite or proto-Canaanite during the Hyksos Dynasty, and therefore the name Resheph is not out of place, as Resheph was one of the main gods of the Hyksos rulers.

During the subsequent New Kingdom era, Resheph worship was suppressed due to his association with the earlier Hyksos dynasty. During the early New Kingdom era, holy texts about Resheph would have been updated to Shed (🔻🏛️📿), which would have been transliterated into Canaanite using the cuneiform script in the late New Kingdom era as ^{deity}šēdu (✳️𐎡), before being translated into Canaanite using the Phoenician script in the early iron age as šdy (𐤆𐤀𐤅), resulting in the confusing 'demonic' (𐡔𐡉𐡃) god in Aramaic.

Nevertheless, neither Marduk, nor Resheph, nor Ablu were similar to the god of Jacob described in Cosmic Genesis. The messengers of Jacob's god were described as climbing a ladder to the sky, parallel to the four sons of Horus the Elder in the Egyptian religion, the enemy of Setekh, indicating that the name Resheph replaced another name in Cosmic Genesis before the time of Moses. The presence of Åwn (𐡍𐡅𐡀) in the Aramaic translation, as well in Samaria according to Hosea, suggests that the Samaritans believed the god of Abraham, who had come from Ur in Sumer, was ^{deity}Ān (✳️✳️), the original Sumerian sky-god, and father of the four winds, which paralleled the role of the four sons of Horus the Elder in Egyptian religion.

The Vetus Latina version of the book, refers to it as the 'Book of Hadassah, which is called Esther,' indicating that the Alpha and Vetus Latina versions originated in Hasidean version of the book of Esther. The Hasideans of the second temple era were a group of Judeans who practiced strict adherence to the laws of Moses found in the Torah, and therefore redacting the name of Moloch to Shadday would have been consistent with their beliefs.

The later use of the term Lord God King in the Vaticanus version, and Lord King, in the Vetus Latina both point to the original god in the text being Moloch, which explains why the Masoretic version was stripped of all reference to any god, and why random substitutions appear to have happened in the other versions. In this case, the Vaticanus' Lord Lord appears to be an intentional mistranslation of the Lord King (Dominus Rex) found later in most copies of the Vetus Latina, and therefore Lord Moloch is used in this translation, as the most likely reconstruction of the original text's meaning.

3 Codex Vaticanus: cyrie o theos o basileus (ΚΥΡΙΕΟΘΕΟC ΟΒΑCΙΛΕΥC). Translation: Lord the God the King

• Septuagint manuscript 319: Cyrie (Κᾱριᵹ). Translation: Lord

• Masoretic Text: section missing

• Codex Monacensis (VL 130): Dominus Rex. Translation: Lord King

The Vetus Latina's Dominus Rex is curious, as it can only be translated back into Aramaic as Lord Melech (ΝͿＬͱ ＾ͱΊＹΝ). The Codex Vaticanus seems to confirm the Aramaic source text used a term like that, as it has a phrase with would translate back as Lord God Melech (ΝͿＬͱ ＬΝ ＾ͱΊＹΝ). The term Lord the god (Κύριος ο θεὸς) is used often in the Septuagint, and appears to be a direct continuation of Adon Elim (ΥＬ⨥ ΥΑ⨥) a Canaanite epithet for El (God), found in the Ugaritic Texts and other ancient sources.

While Lord the god by itself makes sense within the Israelite religions, the addition of King (ﾏﾙﾋﾟ) confuses the situation entirely, as this appears to be the name of the god in question, and this renders as the name Moloch, which is a proper name of a god, that happened to be spelled the same way as the word king in Aramaic: mlka (ﾏﾙﾋﾟ), Hebrew: mlk (מלך), Phoenician: mlk (𐤊𐤋𐤌), and Syriac: mlka (ܡܠܟܐ).

That the Judahites were worshiping a god named Moloch is not debated, King Josiah banned Moloch's worship in 625 BC, when he promoted Yhwh to be the Judahite national god, however, based on the writings of Baruch, it is clear that the Judahites reverted to the old gods after Josiah died. These references to Moloch do make sense in relation to Mordecai's name as Marduk was the king of the Babylonian gods, and so Mordecai was named after the Babylonian version of Moloch. This also explains why the Masoretic version had all references to God stripped from it, as the book was about a prophet of the wrong god.

The additions of the set of names 'Abraham, Isaac, and Jacob,' found in the Vetus Latina version also makes sense, as the translators seem to have been trying to justify Moloch by stating he was the god of the three ancient patriarchs. The Israelites in southern Egypt never stopped using the name Moloch, and carried it south with them into Sudan and Ethiopia, and the Ge'ez (and Amharic) word for 'God' continues to be Ämlak (አምላክ) to this day, derived from the ancient Semitic word for king. As the original meaning of the name translated as King was clearly Moloch, that name is restored in this translation.

4 Codex Vaticanus: basileu tôn theôn (ΒΑCΙΛΕΥΤΩΝ ΘΕΩΝ). Translation: king of gods

- Septuagint manuscript 319: term missing
- Masoretic Text: section missing
- Codex Monacensis (VL 130): term missing

The reference to the 'king of the gods' is only found in the Vaticanus version, however, is clearly a reference to the god Moloch, who was called the 'king of the gods' by his worshipers.

Esther (Vaticanus): Chapter 5

On the third day, when she had ceased praying, she took off her humble dress and put on her glorious apparel. Being splendidly clothed, and having called on God the overseer and preserver of all things, she took her two servers, and she leaned on one, as a delicate female, and the other followed carrying her train. She was blooming in the perfection of her beauty, and her face was cheerful, and it was benevolent, but her heart was straitened for fear.

Having passed through all the doors, she stood before the king. He was sitting on his royal throne, and he had put on all his glorious apparel, covered all over with gold and precious stones, and was very terrible. Having raised his face resplendent with glory, he looked with intense anger, and the queen fell and changed color as she fainted, and she leaned on the head of the girl who went before her.

But God changed the spirit of the king to gentleness, and with great passion, he sprang from off his throne, and took her into his arms, until she recovered, and he comforted her with peaceful words, and said to her, "What is the matter, Esther? I am your brother. Be cheerful, you will not die, for our command is openly declared to you, come close to me."

Having raised the golden scepter he laid it on her neck, and embraced her, and said, "Speak to me."

She said to him, "I saw you, my lord, like a messenger god,[1] and my heart was troubled for fear of your glory, for you, my lord, are to be wondered at, and your face is full of grace."

While she was speaking, she fainted and fell. Then the king was troubled, and all his servants comforted her. The king asked, "What do you want, Esther? What is your request? Ask even half of my kingdom, and it will be yours."

Esther replied, "Today is my great day, if then it seems good to the king, let both him and Haman come to the feast which I will prepare this day."

The king ordered, "Bring Haman here, that we may do as Esther requests."

They both went to the feast which Esther had invited them to. At the banquet, the king said to Esther, "What is your request, Queen Esther? State it, and you will have all that you require."

She answered, "My request and my petition are, if I have found favor in the sight of the king, let the king and Haman come again tomorrow to the feast which I will prepare for them, and tomorrow I will do the same."

Haman left the king very happy and content, but when Haman saw Mordecai the Judahite in the court, he was greatly enraged. Having gone into his own house, he called his friends, and his wife Zosaran.[2] He showed them his wealth, and the glory with which the king had invested him, and how he had caused him to take precedence and carry chief rule in the kingdom. Haman said, "The queen has called no one to the feast with the king but me, and I am invited tomorrow. But this thing did not please me, while I was there, I saw Mordecai the Judahite in the court."

Zosaran his wife and his friends said to him, "Have gallows set up for you, fifty cubits high, and in the morning speak to the king, and let Mordecai be hanged on the gallows. Then you can go to the feast with the king and be happy."

The idea pleased Haman, and so the gallows were prepared.

Esther (Vaticanus): Chapter 5 Notes

1 Codex Vaticanus: angelon Theou (ⲀⲅⲅⲈⲗⲟⲚⲐⲈⲟⲨ).
Translation: messenger god

- Septuagint manuscript 319: angelon Theou (ἀγγόλον θόου). Translation: messenger god

- Masoretic Text: section missing

- Codex Monacensis (VL 130): angelus Dei. Translation: messenger god

2 Codex Vaticanus: Zôsaran (ⲌⲱⲤⲀⲢⲀⲚ)

- Septuagint manuscript 319: Zôsaran (Ζωσᾰρᾰν)

- Aleppo Codex: Zrš (זרש)

- Leningrad Codex: Zeresh (זֶ֫רֶשׁ)

- Codex Monacensis (VL 130): Zosarra

As the names all appear to derive from a common name, however, the Aramaic text is lost, the Greek name is used in this translation.

Esther (Vaticanus): Chapter 6

The Lord would not allow the king to sleep that night, so he told his servant to bring in the books, the records of daily events, to read to him. He found the records written regarding Mordecai, how he had told the king about the two eunuchs of the king when they were keeping guard, and wanted to lay hands on Artaxerxes, and the king asked, "What honor or favor have we done for Mordecai?"

The king's servants answered, "You have not done anything for him."

While the king was inquiring about the kindness of Mordecai, Haman was in the court, and the king asked, "Who is in the court?"

Haman had come to speak to the king, that he should hang Mordecai on the gallows, which he had prepared. The king's servants answered, "Know that Haman stands in the court."

The king ordered, "Call him," and the king asked Haman, "What should I do to a man who I wish to honor?"

Haman thought to himself, 'Who would the king honor other than me?' and so he answered the king, "As for the man who the king wishes to honor, let the king's servants bring the robe of fine linen which the king puts on, and the horse on which the king rides, and let him give it to one of the king's noble friends, and let him adorn the man that the king loves, and let him mount him on the horse, and proclaim through the streets of the city. This should be done to every man that the king honors."

The king said to Haman, "You have answered well. Do this to Mordecai the Judahite, who waits in the palace, and don't let a word of what you have spoken be neglected."

So Haman took the robe and the horse, and clothed Mordecai, and mounted him on the horse, and went through the streets of the city, and proclaimed, "This will be for every man who the king wishes to honor."

Mordecai returned to the palace, but Haman went home crying and covered his head. Haman told Zosaran his wife and his friends what had happened, and they replied to him, "If Mordecai is from the people of the Judahites, and you have begun to be humiliated before him, you will assuredly fall, and you will not be able to withstand him, for the god Zeus[1] is with him."

While they were yet speaking, the eunuchs arrived, to rush Haman to the banquet which Esther had prepared.

Esther (Vaticanus): Chapter 6 Notes

1 Codex Vaticanus: theos zôn (ΘΕΟΣ ΖΩΝ). Translation: god alive

- Septuagint manuscript 319: theon (θεὸν). Translation: god

- Masoretic Text: no god is mentioned in the sentence

- Codex Monacensis (VL 130): no god is mentioned in the sentence

The term found in the Vaticanus version, 'theos Zôn' (θεὸς Ζων), meaning 'God alive,' is similar to the term 'theou Zôntos' (θεου Ζωντος), which translate as 'god living,' found in the 1st Kingdoms, as well as later in the Book of Esther. The Greek term in 1st Kingdoms is mirrored in Masoretic Samuel with the term Elohim chayyim (אֱלֹהִים חַיִּים), meaning, 'god of life,' 'divine bread,' or 'god Lehem,' depending on interpretation, however, there is no reason Haman's wife should be using a term for, or name of, an ancient Israelite or Canaanite god. Moreover, as that term was used later in the Book of Esther, it is clear the translator believed the original author meant something else.

This, therefore, has to be interpreted as a reference to an ancient Greek god, as Haman, who was serving as an ambassador from Macedonia at the time, was no doubt married to a Greek noblewoman.

The name Zôn (Ζων) almost identical to the Doric pronunciation of the name of Zeus: Zan (Ζάν), suggesting that Zosaran was a Dorian. In any event, whatever name was originally in the Aramaic text was removed by the translators of the other three versions, and quite noticeably redacted in the case of the Vetus Latina. In the Vetus Latina, Zosaran states that Mordecai was a prophet but does not specify the god he is a prophet of. Mordecai is not considered a prophet in Rabbinical Judaism, further supporting the origin of the Vetus Latina version in another Israelite group living under the rule of the Greeks.

Esther (Vaticanus): Chapter 7

The king and Haman went to drink with the queen, and the king asked Esther at the banquet on the second day, "What is it, Queen Esther? What is your request, and what is your petition? It will be given to you, up to half of my kingdom."

She answered, "If I have found favor in the sight of the king, let my life be granted to my petition and my people to my request. For both, I and my people are sold for destruction, and pillage, and slavery, both we and our children as slave and slave-women and I did not consent to it, for this is not worthy of the king's palace."

The king demanded, "Who is this that has dared to do this thing?"

Esther answered, "The enemy is Haman, this wicked man."

Haman was troubled before the king and the queen. The king rose from the banquet to go into the garden, and Haman began to beg the queen, for he saw that he was in an evil cause. The king returned from the garden, and Haman had fallen on the bed, begging the queen.

The king demanded, "Will you rape my wife in my house?"

When Haman heard it, he changed his attitude. Bougathan,[1] one of the eunuchs, said to the king, "Know that Haman has also prepared a gallows for Mordecai, who spoke concerning the king, and a gallows of fifty cubits high has been set up in the estate of Haman."

The king said, "Let him be hanged on it," and so Haman was hanged on the gallows that had been prepared for Mordecai, and then the king's anger was appeased.

Esther (Vaticanus): Chapter 7 Notes

1 Codex Vaticanus: Bougathan (ⲃⲟⲩⲅⲁⲑⲁⲛ)

* Septuagint manuscript 319: Agathas (φγᴧθᴧc)

* Aleppo Codex: Ḥrbwnh (חרבונה)

* Leningrad Codex: Charvovnah (חַרְבוֹנָה)

* Codex Monacensis (VL 130): Buzatas

As none of the source texts agree on the name, the Vaticanus version's name is transliterated in this translation.

Esther (Vaticanus): Chapter 8

On that day, King Artaxerxes gave to Esther all that belonged to Haman the slanderer, and Mordecai was called by the king, for Esther had shown that he was related to her. The king took the ring which he had taken away from Haman and gave it to Mordecai, and Esther appointed Mordecai over all that had been Haman's. She spoke yet again to the king, and fell at his feet, and implored him to do away the acts of Haman, and all that he had done against the Judahites. Then the king stretched out to Esther the golden scepter, and Esther rose to stand near the king. Esther said, "If it seems good to you, and I have found favor in your sight, let an order be sent that the letters sent by Haman may be reversed, that was written for the destruction of the Judahites, who are in your kingdom. For how will I be able to watch the slaughter of my people, and how will I be able to survive the destruction of my families?"

The king said to Esther, "If I have given and freely granted you all that was Haman's, and hanged him on a gallows, because he laid his hands on the Judahites, what do you yet further seek? Write it also in my name, as it seems good to you, and seal it with my ring, for whatever orders are written at the command of the king, and sealed with my ring, it is not lawful to go against them."

So the scribes were called in the first month, which is Nisan, on the twenty-third day in the same year, and orders were written to the Judahites, whatever the king had commanded to the local governors and chiefs of the satraps, from India all the way to Kush, 127 satraps, in the several provinces, according to their dialects. They were written by order of the king, and sealed with his ring, and they sent the letters by the posts, in which he ordered them to use their own laws in every city, and to help each other, and to treat their adversaries, and those who attacked them, as they pleased, on one day in all the kingdom of Artaxerxes, on the thirteenth day of the twelfth month, which is Adar. Let the copies be posted in conspicuous places throughout the kingdom, and let all the Judahites be ready on this day to fight against their enemies. The following is a copy of the letter of the orders:

> The great king Artaxerxes sends greetings to the rulers of districts in 127 satrapies, from India to Kush, to all those who are faithful to our interests.

> Many who have been frequently honored by the most abundant kindness of their benefactors have conceived ambitious designs, oftentimes exhortation has made partakers of the guilt of shedding innocent blood, and has involved in irremediable calamities, many of those who had been appointed to offices of authority, who had been entrusted with the management of their friends' affairs,

while, by the false sophistry of an evil disposition, have deceived the simple candor of the ruling powers.

Oftentimes also fair speech of those, that are put in trust to manage their friends' affairs, has caused many that are in authority to be partakers of innocent blood, and has involved them in terrible problems, beguiling with the lies and deceit of their lewd disposition the innocent and good princes.

It is possible to see, not so much from more ancient traditional accounts, as it is immediately in your power to see it by examining what things have been wickedly perpetrated by the baseness of men unworthily holding power, to pay attention with regard to the future, that we may maintain the government in undisturbed peace for all men, adopting needful changes, and ever judging those cases which come under our notice, with a truly equitable decision.

For while Haman the son of Amyntas, a Macedonian,[1] in truth, an alien from the blood of the Persians, and differing widely from our mild course of government, having been hospitably entertained by us, obtained so large a share of our universal kindness, as to be called our father, and to continue the person next to the royal throne, reverenced of all, yet overcome by the pride of his station, endeavored to deprive us of our dominion, and our life. Having by various and subtle methods demanded the destruction of both Mordecai, our deliverer and perpetual benefactor, and Esther the blameless consort of the kingdom, with their

whole nation. By these methods he thought, having sur-
prised us in a defenseless state, to transfer the dominion of
the Persians to the Macedonians. But we find that the Judahites, who have been consigned to destruction by the
most abominable of men, are not malefactors, but living
according to just laws, and being the sons of the highest,
supreme, living God,[2] who gave our ancestors the kingdom
and maintains it in good order.

You will, therefore, do well in refusing to obey the letter
sent by Haman the son of Amyntas, because he who has
done these things, has been hanged with his whole family
at the gates of Susa, the prevailing god[3] had swiftly returned to him a worthy recompense. Having openly published a copy of this letter in every place, to give the Judahites permission to use their own lawful customs, and to
help them, that on the thirteenth of the twelfth month,
Adar, on that day. For God, who rules over all things, has
made this day to be a joy for his chosen people instead of a
day of destruction for them. Therefore, you also shall celebrate this with all good cheer as a holiday among your
commemorative feasts, that both now and from now on it
may be a day of deliverance to us and who are well dis-
posed towards the Persians, but to those that plotted
against us a memorial of destruction. Every city and
satrapy collectively, which will not do so, will be consumed
with vengeance by spear and fire. It will be made not only
inaccessible to men but most hateful to wild animals and
birds forever.

Let the copies be posted in conspicuous places through-out the kingdom and let all the Judahites be ready against this day, to fight against their enemies.

So the horsemen went quickly out to perform the king's commands, and the ordinance was also published in Susa. Mordecai went out robed in the royal apparel and wearing a golden crown, and a diadem of fine purple linen and the people in Susa saw it and rejoiced. The Judahites were happy and celebrated in every city and province wherever the ordinance was published. Wherever the proclamation took place, the Judahites had joy and gladness, feasting and laughter, and many of the nations were circumcised, and became Judahites, in fear of the Judahites.

Esther (Vaticanus): Chapter 8 Note

1 Codex Vaticanus: Macedôn (ΜΑΚΕΔΩΝ). Translation: Macedonian

- Septuagint manuscript 319: Bougaeos (Βουγαιος)

- Masoretic Text: the name is missing

- Codex Monacensis (VL 130): Macedonica

This reference to Haman, confirms that the translators of the Vaticanus and Vetus Latina versions considered the term found in the Aramaic source texts to mean 'Macedonian,' as the translator of the Alpha version translated the term earlier, where the Masoretic texts use the term Agagai (אֲגָגִי). Unlike the earlier reference to Haman in the Vaticanus version, where he was praised, in this case, he is being denounced by the king, and therefore it would have not been objectionable to Ptolemy V and seems to have been left in the text.

The meaning of the word Bougaeos (Βουγαιος) in Alpha version, as well as in chapter 1 of the Vaticanus version where it is used in the same way it is here in the Alpha version, is an unknown term, however, sometimes translated as bully or braggart. As it is used as a substitute for Macedonian in both places, it is likely an attempt to transliterate Brygoe (Βρύγοι) back into Greek from Aramaic. The Brygoe, more commonly called the Bryges in English, were a tribe of people that settled in Macedonia, northern Greece, and Albania shortly before the Persians invaded Greece.

2 Codex Vaticanus: ypsistou megistou zôntos theou (ΥΨΙCΤΟΥ ΜΕΓΙCΤΟΥ ΖΩΝΤΟC ΘΕΟΥ). Translation: highest supreme living god

• Septuagint manuscript 319: mono cae alêthinos Theos (μ𝔵νο և𝔞ι ἀλև̄θιν𝔵c Θ𝔶𝔵ς). Translation: only and true God

• Masoretic Text: the term is missing

• Codex Monacensis (VL 130): excelsis deo. Translation: highest god

The Vaticanus and Vetus Latina versions of Esther both refer to the 'highest God,' suggesting that this was in the Aramaic text that was translated. As Xerxes I was a Zoroastrian, this likely started out as the Zoroastrian title of Ahura Mazda: A-frajdum (افراجـدم) meaning 'Highest.' The full title in the Vaticanus version appears to be the Zoroastrian title A-frajdum Aekh Tan (افراجـدم ائیـک تن) meaning 'Highest Supreme Soul,' which, if the translators still recognized it when the Alpha and Vetus Latina translations were made, would explain their redactions of the name. In any event, if the letter was published in the name of Xerxes, the god being referenced was Ahura Mazda.

As the source texts do not agree on the titles of the god, the titles are translated directly from the Vaticanus version in this translation.

3 Codex Vaticanus: epicratountos theou (ⲉⲡⲓⲕⲣⲁⲧⲟⲩⲛⲧⲟⲥⲑⲉⲟⲩ) Translation: prevailing god

- Septuagint manuscript 319: molis critês (μⲟλιc ⳝⲣⲓⲧⲣc). Translation: just judge

- Masoretic Text: the letter is missing from the chapter

- Codex Monacensis (VL 130): Deus qui scrutatur. Translation: god who examines

Esther (Vaticanus): Chapter 9

In the twelfth month, on the thirteenth day of the month which is Adar, the letters written by the king arrived. On that day the enemies of the Judahites died, no one resisted because of fear of them. The chiefs of the satraps, and the princes and the royal scribes, honored the Judahites, for the fear of Mordecai was on them. The order of the king was in force, that he should be celebrated in all the kingdom. In the city of Susa the Judahites murdered five hundred men,[1] including Pharsannestaen, Delphon, Phasga, Phardatha, Barea, Sarbacha, Marmasima, Arouphaeon, Arsaeon, and Zabouthaethan,[2] the ten sons of Haman the son of Amyntas the Bryge, the enemy of the Judahites, and they plundered their property on the same day, and the number of those who perished in Susa was told to the king.

The king said to Esther, "The Judahites have murdered five hundred men in the city of Susa! What do you think they have done in the rest of the country? What then do you still ask, that it may be done for you?"

Esther said to the king, "Let it be granted to the Judahites, as a gift for them tomorrow, the ten sons of Haman."

He permitted it, and he gave up to the Judahites of the city the bodies of the sons of Haman to hang. The

Judahites assembled in Susa on the fourteenth day of Adar, and murdered three hundred more men, but did not steal their property. The rest of the Judahites who were in the kingdom assembled, and helped one another, and obtained peace from their enemies, as they murdered fifteen thousand of them on the thirteenth day of Adar, but took no spoil. They rested on the fourteenth of the same month, and kept it as a day of rest with joy and gladness. The Judahites in the city of Susa assembled also on the fourteenth day and rested, and they kept also the fifteenth with joy and gladness. On this account it is that the Judahites dispersed in every foreign land keep the fourteenth of Adar as a holy day with joy, sending portions each to his neighbor.

Mordecai wrote these things in a book, and sent them to the Judahites, as many as were in the kingdom of Artaxerxes, both those that were near and those that were far away, to establish these as joyful days, and to keep the fourteenth and fifteenth of Adar, for on these days the Judahites obtained peace from their enemies, and as to the month, which was Adar, in which a change was made for them, from mourning to joy, and from sorrow to a good day, to spend the whole of it in good days of feasting and gladness, sending portions to their friends, and to the poor. The Judahites consented to this as Mordecai had written it, showing how Haman the son of Amyntas the Macedonian fought against them, how he made a decree and cast lots to destroy them completely, also how he went to the king, telling him to hang Mordecai, but all the calamities he tried to bring on the Judahites came on himself, and he was hanged, and his children.

Therefore these days were called Purim, because of the lots, for in their language they are called Purim, because of the words of this letter, and because of all they allowed on this account, and all that happened to them. Mordecai established it, and the Judahites took on themselves, and on their seed, and on those that were joined to them to observe it, neither would they on any account behave differently, but these days were to be a memorial kept in every generation, and city, and family, and province. "These days of the Purim," they said, "Will be kept forever, and their memorial will not fail in any generation."

Queen Esther, the daughter of Aminadab, and Mordecai the Judahite wrote all that they had done, and the confirmation of the letter of Purim. Mordecai and Esther the queen appointed a fast for themselves privately, even at that time also having formed their plan against their own health. Esther established it by a command forever, and it was written for a memorial.

Esther (Vaticanus): Chapter 9 Notes

1 Codex Vaticanus: andras pentacosious (ᴀɴᴅᴘᴀᴄ ᴨᴇɴᴛᴀᴋᴏᴄιᴏʏᴄ). Translation: five hundred men

• Septuagint manuscript 319: andras ephtacosia (ᴀⲛⲁⲣⲁⲥ 6ϫⲧⲁⳙ⸕ⲟⲓⲁ). Translation: seven hundred men

• Aleppo Codex: ḥmš måwt [R] åyš [S] (**אִישׁ [ר] מֵאוֹת חֲמֵשׁ [ס]**). Translation: five hundred [R] men [S]

• Leningrad Codex: chamesh me'ovt ish (חֲמֵשׁ מֵאוֹת אִישׁ). Translation: five hundred men

• Codex Monacensis (VL 130): this section is missing

2 Codex Vaticanus: Pharsannestaen cae Delphôn cae Phasga cae Phardatha cae Barea cae Sarbacha cae Marmasima cae Arouphaeon cae Arsaeon cae Zabouthaethan (ⲫᴀᴘᴄᴀɴɴᴇᴄᴛᴀιɴ ᴋᴀι ᴅᴇʌⲫⲱɴ ᴋᴀι ⲫᴀᴄⲅᴀ ᴋᴀι ⲫᴀᴘᴅᴀⲑᴀᴋᴀιвᴀᴘᴇᴀᴋᴀιᴄᴀᴘвᴀxᴀᴋᴀιᴍᴀᴘᴍᴀᴄιᴍᴀᴋᴀι ᴀᴘᴏʏⲫᴀιᴏɴ ᴋᴀι ᴀᴘᴄᴀιᴏɴ ᴋᴀι ᴢᴀвᴏʏⲑᴀιⲑᴀɴ). Translation: Pharsannestaen and Delphôn and Phasga and Phardatha and Barea and Sarbacha and Marmasima and Arouphaeon and Arsaeon and Zabouthaethan

• Septuagint manuscript 319: Pharsan cae o aderphos tou cae ê Pharna cae ê Gagaphardatha cae ê Marmasaema cae Izathouth (ⲫⲁⲣⲥⲁⲛ ⳙⲁⲓ ⲟ ⲁⲁ6⸕ϩ⸕ⲥ ⲧⲟⲩ ⳙⲁⲓ ⳑ ⲫⲁⲣⲛⲁ ⳙⲁⲓ ⳑ ⲅⲁⳗⲁϩⲁⲣⲁⲁⲑⲁ ⳙⲁⲓ ⳑ ⲙⲁⲣⲙⲁⲥⲁⳙⲙⲁ ⳙⲁⲓ ιⲍⲁⲑⲟⲩⲑ). Translation: Pharsan and his brother and Pharna and Gagaphardatha and Marmasaima and Izathouth

• Aleppo Codex: pršndtå [s] wåt [r] dlpwn [s] wåt [r] åsptå [s] 8 wåt [r] pwrtå [s] wåt [r] ådlyå [s] wåt [r] årydtå [s] 9 wåt [r] prmštå [s] wåt [r] årysy [s] wåt [r] årydy [s] wåt [r] wyztå [s] (פרשנדתא [ס] ואת [ר] דלפון [ס] ואת [ר] אספתא [ס] ואת [ר] ח ואת [ר] פורתא [ס] ואת [ר] אדליא [ס] ואת [ר] אריךתא [ר] ט ואת [ר] פרמשתא [ס] ואת [ס] אריסי [ר]). [ר] ואת [ס] ארידי [ר] ואת [ס] וייתא [ס]). Translation: Pršndtå [S] and [R] Dlpwn [S] and [R] Åsptå [S] 8 and [R] Pwrtå [S] and [R] Ådlyå [S] and [R] Årydtå [S] and [R] Prmštå [S] and [R] Årysy [S] and [R] Årydy [S] and [R] Wyztå [S]

• Leningrad Codex: parshandata ve'et - dalfovn ve'et - aspata ve'et - povrata ve'et - adalya ve'et - aridata ve'et - parmashta ve'et - arisai ve'et - aridai ve'et – vayzata (פַּרְשַׁנְדָּתָא וְאֵת – דַּלְפוֹן וְאֵת – אַסְפָּתָא וְאֵת – פּוֹרָתָא וְאֵת – אֲדַלְיָא וְאֵת – אֲרִידָתָא וְאֵת – פַּרְמַשְׁתָּא וְאֵת – אֲרִיסַי וְאֵת – אֲרִדַי וְאֵת – וַיְזָתָא). Translation: Paršandātā and Dalpôn and Åaspātā and Pôrātā and Ădalyā and Ărîdātā and Parmaštā and Ărîsay and Ăriday and Wayəzātā

• Codex Monacensis (VL 130): this section is missing

Both the Vaticanus and Masoretic versions name ten people, which are implied to be the ten sons of Haman, while the Alpha version names five people, and then states the ten sons of Haman were also killed.

Esther (Vaticanus): Chapter 10

The king levied a tax on his kingdom both by land and sea. As for his strength and valor, and the wealth and glory of his kingdom, look, they are written in the book of the Persians and Medes, for a memorial. Mordecai was viceroy to King Artaxerxes, and was a great man in the kingdom, and honored by the Judahites, and passed his life beloved of all his nation.

Mordecai said, "These things have been done of God. For I remember the dream which I had concerning these matters, for not one particular of them has failed. There was a little fountain which became a river, and there was light, and the sun and a lot of water. The river is Esther, whom the king married, and made queen. The two dragons are myself and Haman. The river are those nations that combined to destroy the name of the Judahites. But as for my nation, this is Israel, even they cried to God and were delivered, for the Lord delivered his people. The Lord rescued us out of all these calamities, and God worked such signs and great wonders as have not been done among the nations. Therefore he ordained two lots. One for the people of God, and one for all the other nations. These two lots came for an appointed season, and for a day of judgment, before God, and for all the nations. God remembered his people and vindicated his inheritance. They will observe these days in the month Adar, on the fourteenth and the fifteenth day of the month, with an assembly, and joy and gladness before God, throughout the generations forever among his people Israel.

Esther (Vaticanus): Postscript

In the fourth year of the reign of Ptolemy and Cleopatra, Dositheos, who he said was a priest and Levite, and Ptolemy his son, brought this letter of Purim, which they said was the same, and that Lysimachus the son of Ptolemy, who was in Jerusalem, had interpreted.

Esther (Alpha): Chapter 1

In the second year of the reign of Xerxes[1] the great king, on the first day of the month of Adar-Nisan[2] (which is Dystros Xandicos), Mordecai[3] the son of Jair the son of Shimei the son of Kish,[4] of the tribe of Benjamin, had a dream. He was a great man, and one of the captives which King Nebuchadnezzar,[5] of Babylon had taken captive from Jerusalem, with Jeconiah.[6]

There was noise and an uproar, thunder and earthquake, and trouble on the land. Then two great dragons[7] came out ready to fight, and from them came a great call, and by their call everything was troubled, and it was a testimony to all peoples, and a day of darkness and gloom, and the chaos of war, and every nation prepared for battle. We cried to the Lord[8] because of the sound of their crying, and there came from a small fountain, a great river. Light[9] and the Sun[10] rose, and the rivers rose and swallowed the honorable.

After Mordecai woke from sleeping, he thought about what the dream meant, and what the Lord[11] was preparing to do. His dream was hidden in his heart, and at every opportunity he was trying to figure it out. Its interpretation became clear to him on the day when Mordecai rested in the courtyard of the king with Astaos[12] and Teresh,[13] the two eunuchs[14] of the king. He overheard their words and their schemes as they were plotting to attack King Xerxes and kill him. After considering it, Mordecai reported them. The king interrogated the two eunuchs and found Mordecai's words were true, and when the eunuchs confessed, they were led away.

King Xerxes inscribed these events, and Mordecai was written about in the records of the king,[15] so these events would be remembered. The king commanded regarding Mordecai that he should serve in the court of the king and be responsible for guarding every door. He assigned to him for this, Haman[16] the son of Amyntas[17] the Macedonian,[18] before all in the presence of the king. However, Haman searched for a way to harm Mordecai and all his people because of what he had said to the king regarding the eunuchs, and because they had been executed.

After these things, in the days of Xerxes the Great, king of the 127 lands from India to Kush[19] that were subject to him. While Xerxes was on the throne of his kingdom, the king held a wine festival for the rulers of the court of the Persians and Medes, and the rulers of the lands[20] under him, so the wealth of the king's glory and the honor of which he boasted be put on display for 180 days. Until the days were completed, the king gave a wine festival for all those found in the city of Susa,[21] both great and small, for seven days inside the king's courtyard, celebrating his deliverance. There were linen and cotton tapestries and with lavender and scarlet embroidered flowers, and an awning hung by linen and purple cords on silver blocks and Parian[22] marble and gilded with gold. There were gold couches on an emerald pavement, and roses all around.

And the gold goblets were each unique, and the wine was royal, which the king drinks. This wine festival was according to law, for so the king had ordered that the will of the men be done.

Queen Amastri[23] made a banquet for the women in the court of the king. It happened on the seventh day, while the king was feeling good from the wine, he told his servants, to bring Queen Amastri to the assembled banquet in her royal diadem, to show her before his army. However, Amastri did not want to do what the king wanted, as informed by the eunuchs.

When the king heard that Amastri denied his will, he was very angry, and rage burned within him! The king asked all the wise men who knew law and justice, what to do with the queen, because she had not been willing to do what the king wanted before the rulers of the Persians and Medes, and all those who were before the king, and those seated among royalty came to him.

The Bryge[24] advised him, saying, "Queen Amastri has not just wronged the king, but also the governors of the

Persians and Medes, and all the people will hear of how she has disobeyed the orders of the king. Therefore, if it pleases our lord and is acceptable to his thinking, let it be written to all the lands and to all the nations, and make it known that Amastri has rejected the words of the king. Let her royal position be given to someone better than her. Let it be known that she is obedient to the voice of the king, and he will do good for all the kingdoms. Then all wives will honor and praise their husbands from the poor to the rich."

The words pleased the heart of the king, and he acted quickly, following this advice.

Esther (Alpha): Chapter 1 Notes

1 Septuagint manuscript 319: Assyeros (ﭏﻮﻮﯕﻮc).
Translation: Ahasuerus (or Xerxes)

• Codex Vaticanus: Artaxerxou (ﭏﭘﭤﭏﮊﭕﭘﮊﮎﮤ).
Translation: Artaxerxes

• Aleppo Codex: Åḥšwrwš (אַחְשׁוּרוֹשׁ). Translation:
Ahasuerus (or Xerxes)

• Leningrad Codex: Achashverosh (אֲחַשְׁוֵרוֹשׁ). Translation:
Ahasuerus (or Xerxes)

• Codex Monacensis (VL 130): Asueri. Translation:
Ahasuerus (or Xerxes)

The debate regarding who the king in the book of Esther is, goes back to before the Vaticanus version was translated in Jerusalem. The Vaticanus version is the two primary source that name Artaxerxes as the king, however, the other source texts list Ahasuerus. Josephus in the late 1st century AD claimed that Artaxerxes (Ἀρταξέρξου) was the Greek translation of Ahasuerus (אחשורוש), a view repeated in Josippon in the late 10th century, and the Esther Rabbah in the late 11th century, nevertheless, it is not actually correct, as the Greek name Xerxes (Ξέρξης) and Hebrew name Ahasuerus (אחשורוש), both derive from the Persian Xshaya-rsha (𐎧𐏁𐎹𐎠𐎼𐏁𐎠).

The Greek is derived directly from the Persian, while the Hebrew is derived from the Babylonian Aḥshiyarshu (𒄴𒅆𒐼𒅈𒋗). As the Vaticanus version of Esther was likely translated around 181 BC, and in Jerusalem, it is even less likely that the translator would have known the origin of the various names of the Persian kings, and likely just picked the Greek name that was the most similar-sounding to the name in the Aramaic texts that were being translated.

There were four Persian kings name Artaxerxes: Artaxerxes I who reigned between 465 and 424 BC, Artaxerxes II Mnemon who reigned between 404 and 358 BC, Artaxerxes III Ochus who reigned between 358 and 338 BC, and Artaxerxes IV Arses who reigned between 338 and 336 BC. There were two Persian kings named Xerxes: Xerxes I who reigned between 486 and 465 BC, and Xerxes II who reigned for 45 days in 424 BC.

The Vaticanus, Vetus Latina, and Masoretic versions of Esther all refer to the 12th year of Artaxerxes/Ahasuerus reign removing the possibility of this king being either Artaxerxes IV Arses or Xerxes II, neither of which ruled for 12 years. Three of the source texts also mention that he ruled from India (Sindhu) to Kush (Aethiopia), which further reduces the number of possible kings, as Artaxerxes II never ruled Egypt, it had broken away when he assumed the throne, and remained independent for 60 years until Artaxerxes III reconquered them in 343 BC, ten years before Alexander conquered Egypt into his Macedonian Empire. This leaves the kings Xerxes I, Artaxerxes I, and Artaxerxes III as the possible kings of the Book of Esther.

The general modern view is that the king in Esther is Xerxes I, as many of the names in the story are attested in his court, however, the story itself is generally considered fiction. This would place the events of the story between 484 and 474 BC. He had inherited the Persian Empire from Darius I at its greatest extent. It is not clear how much of the world was considered under Persian rule at the time, as Darius had campaigned in Egypt, India, and Greece. He even attempted to conquer the Scythians, and marched his army into the Balkans, and then north around the Black Sea before capturing Crimea.

The Vaticanus version of Esther specifically names the king in the book Artaxerxes, however, the other source texts agree that this was Ahasuerus (אחשורוש / Ασσερος / Asuerus), not Artaxerxes (Αρταξέρξου). As the name Artaxerxes appears to have been adopted in the Classical era by translators due to its phonetic similarity to Ahasuerus, however, Ahasuerus was the name of Xerxes, the name Xerxes is used in this translation. The Alpha versions of Esther specifically names the king in the book Ahasuerus (Ασσερος), not Artaxerxes (Αρταξέρξου). As the name Ahasuerus was the Babylonian name of Xerxes, the name Xerxes is used in this translation.

2 Septuagint manuscript 319: Adar Nisa (ΑΔαⲛⲃ Νισⲇ).
Translation: Adar-Nisan

- Codex Vaticanus: Nisa (Νιⲥⲇ). Translation: Nisan
- Masoretic Text: section missing
- Codex Monacensis (VL 130): Nisan. Translation: Nisan

ESTHER (ALPHA): CHAPTER 1 NOTES

The months of Adar (אדר) and Nisan (נִיסָן) are the last and first month of the ecclesiastical year in the Hebrew calendar. They happen during February, March, and April in the Gregorian Calendar. The names of the month, like the rest of the calendar, was adopted by the Judahites during the Babylonian captivity.

In ancient Babylonian (Akkadian Cuneiform) the months were known as Addaru (𒌓) and Nisānu (𒊺), and the names were in use since at least the second millennium BC. In the Torah, which predates the Babylonian captivity, the month of Nisan was known as Åbyb (אביב / 𐤀𐤁𐤉𐤁), its old Canaanite name. The Book of Esther is the earliest Judahite work that uses the name Nisan, although it did become the common name of the month in the Babylonian Talmud, which was written in Babylonian Aramaic.

The reference to Adar-Nisan (Αδάρ Νισα) found in the Alpha Texts is odd. The Alpha Texts then has a scribal note added by the translator clarifying that this is the month of 'Dystros Xandicos' (Δύστρος Ξανδικός). The Vetus Latina also has this scribal note, which clarifies that Nisan is the month of Andicus, which is a Latin transliteration of Xanthicos (Ξανθικός). Both Dystros (Δύστρος) and Xandicos (Ξανδικός) are names of months on the Macedonian calendar, which was the official calendar of Alexander's Empire, and continued in the Seleucid Empire after he died. In Egypt, the Ptolemys adopted the Egyptian Civil Calendar, and renamed the Egyptian months the names of months found in the Athenian calendar.

This, therefore, proves that the original Greek text of the Alpha Texts, as well as the Greek language source-text for the Vetus Latina, were both translated in either Alexander's Empire, or the subsequent Seleucid Empire. The Alpha Texts's version of the month, 'Adar-Nisan' (Αδάρ Νισα) which is 'Dystros-Xandicos' (Δύστρος Ξανδικός), is a curiosity. Adar-Nisan is not a month, however, may be an archaic attempt to refer to Ådar B (אדר ב'), the second month of Adar that falls between Ådar Å (אדר א') and Nisan in leap years. The Hebrew calendar was derived from the Babylonian calendar, which was itself a descendant of the Akkadian calendar, which in turn was descended from the Sumerian calendar used in Ur.

It is a lunisolar calendar, with 12 lunar months each year, and an additional intercalary month every two or three years, for a total of seven leap years every 19 years. The calendar was in use among the various nations of Mesopotamia since at least the 3rd millennium BC, however, it is believed the intercalary month was added during the Old Babylonian Empire, in the early 2nd millennium BC. The Hebrew name Nisan is derived from the Akkadian Nissan (𒁾). The Sumerians had previously called the month Bar (𒁇). The Hebrew name Adar is likewise derived from the Akkadian Addari (𒊺), which the Sumerians likewise pronounced as She (𒊺). This second month of Adar was established in the Babylonian calendar long before the Judahites were taken captive by Nebuchadnezzar, and was called Addaru Arku (𒊺𒈜𒌁). It is unclear what the Judahites would have called it in the early Persian era, when the book it set.

If this strange month name of Adar-Nisan was in the original Aramaic text, and referred to the second month of Adar, directly before Nisan, then its removal from subsequent translations makes sense, as the Greeks and Latins did not use an intercalary month, and would not have known what this term referred to. If this is the case, then the Alpha version appears to be the oldest translation of Esther, and done within the Seleucid Empire. The Vetus Latina version of Esther, which is not standardized, also appears to be derived from a Greek translation made within the Seleucid Empire, but not the Alpha version. The Vaticanus version claims to have been translated in Jerusalem, however, is missing the strange name, and instead refers to Nisan (Νισα), which would make sense for a Judean translator in Jerusalem under Greek rule, as the text was being prepared for Ptolemy and Cleopatra, who would not have cared about whether it was a leap year or not.

It is worth noting that the year was reported in Esther was the second year of the king's reign, which would be 485 BC if this was Xerxes I, which was a leap year on the Old Babylonian calendar.

3 Septuagint manuscript 319: Mardochaeos (Μᾰβ̌λοχᾰιος)

- Codex Vaticanus: Mardochaeos (Μᴀρᴧοχᴧιος)

- Aleppo Codex (chapter 2): Mrdky (מרדכי)

- Leningrad Codex (chapter 2): Maredechai (מָרְדֳּכַי)

- Codex Monacensis (VL 130): Mardocheus

This name is believed to be a translation of the Neo-Babylonian name Marduka (𒀭𒂞𒌑𒀞), which is found in the Persian court records at Persepolis from the reign of kings Darius I and Xerxes I. Several people in the court had this name, and the Persian records do not clearly identify any as having the same story and position as Mordecai.

This name is considered evidence for the early composition of the Book of Esther, regardless of whether it was factual or fictional. The Persian name Marduka was itself a transliteration of the Old Babylonian name [deity]Marduk (𒀭𒀫𒌓), which was the name of the Babylonian god called Bel in the Book of Daniel. The title Bel translates as Lord, however, the title was applied to many gods by the Babylonians. The most common god called Bel, was Marduk, the solar-calf god. The English name Mordecai is derived from the Hebrew name.

The Mordecai in the book of Esther was said to have been born in Babylon, which would explain his having a Babylonian name. It is also evidence that the book likely originated in the early Persian era, as by the latePersian era, Ezra was already trying to purge the non-Judean elements from the country, including the Israelite priesthoods he did not like. By the late Persian era, no one would have written a fictional story about a Judean named after Marduk.

4 Septuagint manuscript 319: Mardochaeos ho tou Iaeiros tou Semiou tou Cisaeou (ΜΑρͷοχᴧιος ο του ιᴧϭιρος του cϭμϭιου του Κισᴧιου). Translation: Mardochaeos the of Iaerou of Semiou of Cisaeou

• Codex Vaticanus: Mardochaeos ho tou Iaerou tou Semiou tou Cisaeou (ΜΑρͷοχᴧιος ο ΤΟΥ ιᴧιρΟΥ ΤΟΥ cΕΜΕιΟΥ ΤΟΥ ΚιcᴧιΟΥ). Translation: Mardochaeos the of Iaerou of Semiou of Cisaeou

• Aleppo Codex (chapter 2): mrdky bn yảyr bn šmôy bn qyš (מרדכי בן יאיר בן שמעי בן קיש). Translation: Mrdky the son of Yayr the son of Shmay the son of Qysh

• Leningrad Codex (chapter 2): maredochai ben ya'ir ben-shim'i ben-kish (מָרְדֳּכַי בֶּן יָאִיר בֶּן־שִׁמְעִי בֶּן־קִישׁ). Translation: Maredochai the son of Yaair the son of Shimai the son of Kish

• Codex Monacensis (VL 130): Mardocheus filius Iair filii Semei filii Esuus. Translation: Mardocheus son of Iair son of Semei son of Esuu

Mordecai's lineage is repeated verbatim in the second chapter of the Vaticanus and Alpha versions, where he is introduced again, suggesting that the Vaticanus and Alpha versions may have been partially synchronized with the Masoretic version at some point. As the Greek and Latin names are translations of Hebrew or Aramaic versions of the name, the Hebrew version is used in this translation.

5 Septuagint manuscript 319: Nabouchodonosor
(Νᴧⳙⲟυχοᴧοɴοσοϼ)

• Codex Vaticanus: Nabouchodonosor
(ΝᴀʙΟΥΧΟᴧΟΝΟⲤΟϼ)

• Aleppo Codex: Nbwkdnṣr (נבוכדנצר)

• Leningrad Codex: Nevuchadnetzar (נְבוּכַדְנֶאצַּר)

• Codex Monacensis (VL 130): Nabuchodonosor

Nebuchadnezzar II was the king of Babylonia that conquered the kingdom of Judah in 587 BC, and according to both the Judahite and Babylonian records, took a large number of Judahites back to Babylonia as a subject people. These people were released from captivity 48 years later when King Cyrus II of Persia conquered the Babylonian Empire.

6 Septuagint manuscript 319: Iechonios (Ιⳙχοɴⳤᴧⲥ)

• Codex Vaticanus: Iechoniou (ΙⳏΧΟΝΙΟΥ)

• Aleppo Codex (in Chapter 2): Yknyh (יכניה)

• Leningrad Codex (in Chapter 2): Yechaneyah (יְכָנְיָה)

• Codex Monacensis (VL 130): Iechoniam

According to the Babylonian Chronicles and several Judahite books, King Jeconiah of Judah was taken captive by Nebuchadnezzar in 598 BC, and Judah was thereafter ruled by Jeconiah's uncle Zedekiah until Zedekiah's siding with the Egyptians in 587 BC and the kingdom of Judah's destruction. Jeconiah is also recorded in Neo-Babylonian records as Ya'u-kīnu (𒀀𒅀𒌑𒆠𒉡) the king of Yahudu, specifically in the Jehoiachin's Rations Tablets, dated to 592 BC.

7 Septuagint manuscript 319: dracontes (Δραγμιοντόϲ). Translation: dragons (or monsters, beasts)

• Codex Vaticanus: dracontes (ΔΡΑΚΟΝΤΕϹ). Translation: dragons (or monsters, beasts)

• Masoretic Text: section missing

• Codex Monacensis (VL 130): dracones. Translation: dragons (or snakes, serpents)

8 Septuagint manuscript 319: cyrios (Λϲϙβιοϲ). Translation: lord

• Codex Vaticanus: theon (ΘΕΟΝ). Translation: god

• Masoretic Text: section missing.

• Vetus Latina (chapter 2): deus. Translation: god

The words god (אֵל or אֱלֹהִים) and lord (אֲדוֹנִי or בַּעַל) are not mentioned in the Masoretic version of Esther; the Hebrew version is entirely non-religious. In the other three texts the terms 'god' (θεόν / deus) and 'lord' (κύριος / dominus) are used interchangeably. The Vaticanus and Vetus Latina versions of Esther also contains the term Lord the god (Κύριε o θεὸς / Dominus deus) in more than one location. The Vetus Latina also uses the terms Highest Lord (excelsis dominus) and Highest God (excelsis deo). All these terms are translations of Aramaic and Persian terms, yet missing from the Masoretic version, implying that version was seriously altered when it was translated into Hebrew.

9 Septuagint manuscript 319: phôs (ϕοοσ̄). Translation: light

- Codex Vaticanus: phôs (ϕωϲ). Translation: light

- Masoretic Text: section missing.

- Codex Monacensis (VL 130): lux. Translation: light

This reference to the light and the sun rising is a reference to the light that rises before and sets after the sun each day. In ancient times, when the world was believed to be flat, the fact that the sky lightened before the sun broke over the horizon was viewed as proof that there was a sphere of light around the sun. This is now known to be caused by light hitting the upper atmosphere before the lower atmosphere, and the shape of the earth making it resemble a sphere.

The Greeks typically called this light the Eos (Ἔως), while the Romans called this light Aurora, and the Canaanites had called this light Shahar (𐤔𐤄𐤅), all of which mean 'dawn,' however, all the existing translations do not call it dawn, but simply specify light. This implies a Zoroastrian influence on the author, which would place the original composition during the Persian era.

10 Septuagint manuscript 319: Hêlios (Hλιoc). Translation: Helios (or sun)

- Codex Vaticanus: hêlios (HλIOC). Translation: sun (or Helios)

- Masoretic Text: section missing.

- Codex Monacensis (VL 130): Sol. Translation: Sol (or sun)

11 Septuagint manuscript 319: dynastou (Δυναγγοτου). Translation: lord (or master, ruler)

- Codex Vaticanus: theon (ΘΕΟΝ). Translation: god

- Masoretic Text: section missing.

- Vetus Latina (chapter 2): deus. Translation: god

The Greek translation dynastou (δυνάστου), was used in the Septuagint to translate the term avir (אֲבִיר), meaning knight, cavalier, nobleman, noble, stallion, gallant, courageous, or strong, suggesting that this was word was in the original translation.

12 Septuagint manuscript 319: Astaos (φ/στλoc)

- Codex Vaticanus: Gabatha (ΓΑΒΑΘΑ)

- Aleppo Codex (in Chapter 2): Bgtn (בגתן)

- Leningrad Codex (Chapter 2): Bigtan (בִּגְתָ֑ן)

- Vetus Latina (Chapter 2): Bartageus

The name's language of origin and meaning are unclear, however, it may be Sanskrit. The difficulty figuring out the language and meaning of the name is compounded by the fact that the source texts use different transliterations of the original name. Given the diversity of names in the sources, the name Astaos is transliterated directly in this translation from the Alpha version.

13 Septuagint manuscript 319: Thedeutes (ΘϵΔϵυτϵϲ)

- Codex Vaticanus: Tharrha (ΘΑρρΑ)

- Aleppo Codex (in Chapter 2): Trš (תרש)

- Leningrad Codex (Chapter 2): Teresh (תֶּרֶשׁ)

- Vetus Latina (Chapter 2): Thedestes

Unlike the first eunuch's name, this one is fairly similar in the source texts, and is believed to be derived from the Old Persian for 'desire.' Given that most scholars agree on the language and meaning of the name, the common translation of Teresh is used in this translation.

14 Septuagint manuscript 319: eunouchôn (ϵυΝοϊϐχοοΝ).

Translation: eunuchs

- Codex Vaticanus: eunouchôn (ϵΥΝΟΥΧωΝ). Translation: eunuchs

• Aleppo Codex (in Chapter 2): srysy (סריסי). Translation: eunuch (or castrated, neuter)

• Leningrad Codex (Chapter 2): sarisei (סָרִיסֵי). Translation: eunuch (or castrated, neuter)

• Vetus Latina (Chapter 2): eunuchus. Translation: eunuch (or castrated man)

All of the sources use terms meaning 'eunuchs,' however, this is likely a Persian era mistranslation, when the Aramaic term srys (𐡎𐡉𐡓𐡎) was used as the translation for the Neo-Babylonian term ša rēši (𒊭𒊑𒅆), meaning eunuch, vizier, noble, gentleman, or homosexual. This suggests the existence of a Neo-Babylonian precursor to the Aramaic book of Esther.

15 Based on the year recorded for this event in the Vaticanus version, this event would date to 484 BC if the king was Xerxes I, and so the events are likely related to revolts in Babylonia that year. In the summer 484 BC, two Babylonians led revolts against Persian rule. Shamash-eriba was recognized as king in the city of Sippar, in northern Babylonia, and within weeks Bel-shimanni was recognized as king in the towns of Borsippa and Dilbat in southern Babylonia.

Bel-shimanni's revolt only lasted a few weeks, however, Shamash-eriba's revolt wasn't crushed until the following spring. As the assassination plot of the two eunuchs must have been related to either another monarch seizing the throne, or a rebellion within the empire, this timing does correlate with what was happening in the Persian Empire in Xerxes I's second year.

16 Septuagint manuscript 319: Aman (Ἀμὰν)

- Codex Vaticanus: Aman (ᴀᴍᴀɴ)

- Aleppo Codex (in Chapter 3): Hmn (המן)

- Leningrad Codex (Chapter 3): Haman (הָמָן)

- Vetus Latina (Chapter 3): Aman

This name is believed to be a transliteration of the Persian name Imanish (𐎡𐎶𐎴𐎡𐏁), which shows up in ancient Persian records from the era, as well as Greek records from the era as Omanus (Ὀμανυς). As the Hebrew-derived name Haman is the most common, and the Greek and Latin variants are virtually identical, the common name Haman is used in this translation. If this was the son of King Amyntas I of Macedonia, his father was dead before the story began, and his brother Alexander I was the hyparchos of Achaemenid Macedonia in year 2 of Xerxes I. In year 7, when Haman is elevated above everyone else in the court, 479 BC, the Persians lost control of the Greek mainland, and Alexander I became their most important ally in Greece.

If the king of the story was Xerxes I's son Artaxerxes I, then Alexander I was still the king of Macedonia for the first 11 years of Artaxerxes reign, however, was no longer an ally of the Persians after the Greeks captured the fortified Persian port town of Eion, in southern Macedonia, in 474 BC. There is no way to correlate the reference to a Macedonian prince in the Persian court in the era of Artaxerxes III, nor was Aigai the capital of Macedonia after 399 BC, so the reference to it would have been anachronistic. In the letter in chapter 8, the king refers to Haman as being like a father to him, which confirms that Haman was older than the king.

17 Septuagint manuscript 319: Amadathou (Ἀμαδάθου)

• Codex Vaticanus: Amadathou (ΑΜΑΔΑΘΟΥ)

• Aleppo Codex (in Chapter 3): hmdtå (המדתא)

• Leningrad Codex (Chapter 3): Hammedata (הַמְּדָתָא)

• Vetus Latina (Chapter 8): Medadatum

This appears to be a reference to King Amyntas I (Ἀμύντας), the vassal king of Achaemenid Macedonia under 512 to 498 BC. When he died, his son Alexander I became the hyparchos of Achaemenid Macedonia, after the full independence of Macedonia in 479 BC, became its king. This person, Amyntas, is also recorded as being a Macedonas (Μακεδόνας), and a Agagai (אֲגָגִי), in the various versions of Esther, both of which point to his being a Macedonian. The capital of Achaemenid Macedonia was the town of Aigae (Αἰγαί). This is clearly the interpretation that the translator of the Alpha version made when he interpreted Agagai as Macedonian.

Amyntas I died before the story began regardless of who the king was, however, if it was King Xerxes I, the reference to Haman being elevated above everyone else in year 7 makes sense because in Xerxes I's seventh regal year the Persians lost control of the Greek mainland, and Amyntas I's son Alexander I of Macedon became the Persians most important ally on the Greek mainland, and so his brother would have been important at the Persian court. Alexander I was still the king of Macedonia under Xerxes I's heir Artaxerxes I, however, was no longer an ally of Persia, and so it seems unlikely his brother would have had much influence under Artaxerxes I. There is no way to correlate the reference to a Macedonian prince in the Persian court in the era of Artaxerxes III, nor was Aigai the capital of Macedonia after 399 BC, so the reference to it would have been anachronistic.

The Latin name Medadatum appears to be a corruption of the Hebrew name Hammedata (הַמְּדָתָא) found earlier in Masoretic Esther. It seems the Aramaic spelling of the Macedonian name and relative obscurity of the Macedonian's king resulted in the Greek and Hebrew translators not recognizing it and simply transliterating the name. This is not unexpected given that even Xerxes' name was no longer recognized, and the Macedonian pronunciation of the name is still lost today, nevertheless, the references are clear that this was King Amyntas I, and so his name is restored in this translation.

18 Septuagint manuscript 319: Macedôn (ΜΔᏞᏮᏴᎷ).

Translation: Macedonian

- Codex Vaticanus: Bougaeos (ʙᴏΥΓѦɪᴏᴄ)

- Aleppo Codex (in Chapter 3): Åggy (אַגָגִי)

- Leningrad Codex (Chapter 3): Agagai (אֲגָגִי)

- Codex Monacensis (VL 130): name not included in the text

The meaning of the word Macedonian (Μακεδών) in the Alpha version is clear enough, however, the meaning of the word Bougaeos (Βουγαιος) in Vaticanus version, as well as later in chapter 8 of the Alpha version where it is used in the same way it is here in the Vaticanus version, is an unknown term. It is sometimes translated as bully or braggart, as it is similar to a word in Archaic Greek that is translated that way. Here it is used as a substitute for Macedonian in both places, and it is likely an attempt to transliterate Brygoe (Βρύγοι) back into Greek from Aramaic. The Brygoe, more commonly called the Bryges in English, were a tribe of people that settled in Macedonia, northern Greece, and Albania shortly before the Persians invaded Greece.

The term used in the Masoretic version is generally accepted as the name of a tribe, and is often assumed to be descended from the ancient Amalekite king Agag from the time of King Saul. An alternate theory is that Agagai (אֲגָגִי) is a reference to Aigae (Αἰγαὶ), the capital of Macedonia before 399 BC. This was clearly the way the translators of the Alpha version interpreted the word, resulting in the term Macedonians. The translators of both the Vaticanus and Vetus Latina versions also later referred to Haman as being a Macedonian, and all three sources other than the Masoretic versions include a letter that refers to Haman as involved in a Macedonian plot to destabilize the Persian Empire.

Clearly, the translator of the Vaticanus version did not want to offend the monarchs he was preparing the translation for, and so transliterated the word Bougaeos instead of translating it in this section of text where the Macedonian was being praised. It is worth noting that early in his reign, Ptolemy V had fought a major war against the Macedonians, and lost. Mentioning them in the book the translator was preparing for Ptolemy V and Cleopatra I would have not been well received, which would explain why he transliterated the word instead of translating it as Macedonian.

19 Septuagint manuscript 319: Indicês cae Aithiopias (ινⲆⲓⲕⲏⲥ ⲕⲁⲓ Ⲁⲓⲑⲓⲟⲡⲫⲁⲥ). Translation: Indian and Aethiopian

• Codex Vaticanus: Indicês (ινⲆⲓⲕⲏⲥ). Translation: Indian

• Aleppo Codex: hdw wôd kwš (הדו ועד כוש). Translation: Indus and up to Kush

• Leningrad Codex: hoddu ve'ad-kush (הֹדּוּ וְעַד־כּוּשׁ). Translation: Indus and up to Kush

• Codex Monacensis (VL 130): India usque Aethiopiam. Translation: India and Aethiopia

All four source texts list India (or the Sindhu River) as one end of the Persian Empire, however, only three source texts list Kush (Aethiopia) at the other end. The Vaticanus version is the one version that does not mention Kush (Aethiopia) in this section of text, and instead simply says "from India."

It is later mentioned in the letter in chapter 8. The omission of Kush from the opening chapter of the Vaticanus translation was likely intentional. It is known that Ptolemy V, who was likely the Ptolemy the Vaticanus version was translated for, disliked the Kushites. It is believed that they became involved in the dynastic struggles in Egypt during Ptolemy IV, which caused Ptolemy V to dislike them, however, the exact events are unknown today.

Nevertheless, if this translator in Jerusalem wanted King Ptolemy V to read his work, he would not have mentioned the Kushites. After Ptolemy VI briefly occupied the Nubian lands in between Egypt and Kush, there is little evidence of the later Ptolemys having any contact with Kush, which supports Ptolemy V and Cleopatra I being the Ptolemy and Cleopatra mentioned in the postscript, and the year of translation as 181 BC. It is also worth noting that the number of 127 lands is consistent across the source texts, although it is not clear what this relates to exactly. The empire was divided into 36 satrapies (provinces) by Darius I, however, the satrapies were also subdivided into smaller districts, and it is not known how many of those there were. This is generally assumed to be a reference to those districts. As Aethiopia was the Greek name for Kush, the name of Kush, which would have been used in the original, Kush is restored in this translation.

20 Septuagint manuscript 319: chôres (χῶρός). Translation: lands

• Codex Vaticanus: satrapôn (сатратιωN). Translation: satrapies (provinces)

• Aleppo Codex: mdynwt (מדינות). Translation: countries, lands, provinces, regions

• Leningrad Codex: medinovt (מְדִינוֹת). Translation: countries, lands, provinces, regions

• Codex Monacensis (VL 130): does not mention the governors of the empire being invited, just those in Susa Thebari

It is unclear why the Vetus Latina deviates so much here, as it both have the deviation of "twelfth year," instead of "third year," and does not mention the satraps being present. The other three source texts mention the governors of the satrapies being present, and the Vaticanus version even maintains the Persian name, which does support its authenticity on this issue.

21 Septuagint manuscript 319: Sousoes tê poli (Cοⲑⲥⲟⲓⲥ ⲧⲗⲓ πⲟⲗϭⲓ). Translation: Susa the city

- Codex Vaticanus: Sousoes tê poli (ⲥⲟⲩⲥⲟⲓⲥⲧⲏⲓⲡⲟⲗⲉⲓ). Translation: Susa the city

- Aleppo Codex: Šwšn hbyrh (שׁוּשַׁן הַבִּירה). Translation: Susa the capital, Susa the citadel

- Leningrad Codex: Shushan habbirah (שׁוּשַׁן הַבִּירָה). Translation: Susa the capital, Susa the citadel

- Codex Monacensis (VL 130): Susis Thebari

Susa was the ancient Elamite capital city, which was conquered by the Persian king Cyrus II in 540 BC. Under his heir Cambyses II, Susa became one of the four capitals of the Persian Empire. Under Darius I the city was expanded as the winter capital, while Persepolis to the east was the summer capital. This situation continued under Xerxes I, and for the rest of the Persian Empire. The city did not begin declining until after the conquest of Alexandria.

The variation found in the Vetus Latina is a Latin transliteration of the Greek Sousoes tê bari (Σούσοις Τη Βάρε) which means being 'Susa the capital,' and is itself proof that the Vetus Latina was translated from a Greek source. This is consistent with the Hebrew Shushan habbirah (שׁוּשַׁן הַבִּירָה), which also means Susa the Capital. This was Susa's status from Cambyses II's reign until the Macedonians conquered the Persian Empire.

The use of the terms polei (πόλει) in both the Vaticanus and Alpha versions could also be interpreted as 'fortified capital,' but is ambiguous, and could simply mean town, as it is generally translated. The Acropolis in Athens was an example of the term polis specifically referring to the capital, in this case, the 'high town' above the city. The capital buildings in Alexandria were also called the Polis in the Ptolemy's Egypt. Therefore, the term Polis is translated as 'capital city' in this translation, as all four source texts indicate that was in the original text.

22 Septuagint manuscript 319: Parinou (παρβ̸ν̸ου).

Translation: Parian

• Codex Vaticanus: Parinou (ΠΑΡΙΝΟΥ). Translation: Parian

• Aleppo Codex: ômwdy (עמודי). Translation: pillar

• Leningrad Codex: ammudei (עַמּוּדֵי). Translation: pillar

• Codex Monacensis (VL 130): Paros

Parian Marble was from the Island of Paros in the Aegean Sea. It was highly prized by the Greeks, and many ancient statues were carved in it, including the Winged Victory of Samothrace. The mines of Paros were in use since at least the 6th century BC.

23 Septuagint manuscript 319: Ouastin (Ουἀστιν)

- Codex Vaticanus: Astin (ᴀᴄᴛɪɴ)

- Aleppo Codex: Wšty (וֹשְׁתִי)

- Leningrad Codex: Vashti (וַשְׁתִּי)

- Codex Monacensis (VL 130): Vasthi

If the king in Esther was Xerxes I, then this queen would have most likely been Amāstrī (𒄠𒈦𒋫𒊑𒅖), known in Greek records from the era as Amestris (Ἄμηστρις), Ámāstris (Ἄμαστρις), or Amastrinē (Ἀμαστρινε). Xerxes I was already married to Amastri before Darius I died. It had been a political wedding, as her father Otanes had been one of the seven Persians that helped Xerxes I kill his predecessor King Bardiya (or a magical doppelganger named Gaumata) and seize the Persian throne. She lived a long time, and is believed to have died in 424 BC, probably at more than 80 years old. The ancient Greeks accused her of making human sacrifices to Hades in order to live so long, however, there is no evidence of human sacrifice in the Persian Empire, and Persian law expressly forbade it.

Conversely, if this was the queen of King Artaxerxes I, it would have been Queen Damaspia. While Artaxerxes I did take additional wives, he appears to have remained close to Damaspia until they both died in 424 BC, while traveling together. If this was Artaxerxes III, then it was probably Atossa, however, little is known about their relationship.

As this story appears to be about Xerxes I, whose name was forgotten by the time of the various translations were made, it is understandable that the name of his wife was also no longer understood by the time the translations were made, and therefore the Persian name Amastri is used in this translation.

24 Septuagint manuscript 319: Bougaeos (Βουγαιος)

- Codex Vaticanus: Mouchaeos (ΜΟΥΧΑΙΟC)

- Aleppo Codex: mwmkn [mmwkn] (מומכן [ממוכן])

- Leningrad Codex: mumechan K [memuchan Q] (מוּמְכָן כ [מְמוּכָן ק])

- Codex Monacensis (VL 130): Mordecai

None of the names is a close match, and again, as in the previous name list, Modecai is present in the Vetus Latina, but not the other source texts. The Masoretic name Mumechan / Memuchan (מוּמְכָן / מְמוּכָן) is identical to the name Memuchan (מְמוּכָן) from the previous name list of Persian and Median officials, other than the different vowel points and accents added by the Masorites to the K variant, and this is probably intended to represent the same person. The Vaticanus' name Mouchaeos (Μουχαιος) appears from nowhere, and may be an attempt to transliterate the name Memuchan (מְמוּכָן) into Greek. If so, Mouchaeos may have once been part of the list of three officials found in the Vaticanus' version, however, it is equally possible that the translation of the Masoretic version simply added Memuchon to the previous list of officials in order to clarify who this person was, and why they were suddenly talking to the king.

The Alpha version's Bougaeos (Βουγαιος) appears from nowhere but is less conspicuous as the Alpha version did not include a list of who the king was talking to. The name Bougaeos is also unrelated to the various names in all three of the previous lists of officials. The term Bougaeos appears to be derived from an Aramaic translation of Bryges (Βρύγοι), as the word is used interchangeably with Macedonian (Μακεδών), and so its possible the text was referring to the 'Macedonian/Bryge' speaking to the king, but it seems unlikely the person would not have been named, however, could be interpreted as Haman speaking.

The Vetus Latina inclusion of Mordecai again, and having him make the suggestion to the king to punish the Queen seems out of place in the overall narrative of the story, as does him being one of the Persian and Median officials. It seems the intent of the translator of the Vetus Latina version of Esther was to elevate Mordecai, who in Rabbinical Judaism is considered less important than Esther in the book of Esther. As the names don't correlate, the translation of Bryge is used in this translation.

Esther (Alpha): Chapter 2

It was established as a tradition regarding Amastri, and what she had done to King Xerxes. Then the servants of the king said, "Let us search for beautiful virgins, and let be placed under the charge of Hegai[1] the eunuch, the guard of the women. Then whichever girl is pleasing to the king will be appointed to replace Amastri." Then they quickly followed through.

There was a Judahite[2] in the city of Susa, and his name was Mordecai ben Jair ben Shimei ben Kish, of the tribe of Benjamin. He had faithfully raised Esther, the daughter of his father's brother. The child was beautiful in appearance and lovely to see, and the girl was taken to the palace of the king. When Hagai the eunuch who guarded, saw the girl, she was more pleasing than all the other women. Esther found his personal favor and compassion, so he rushed to take charge of her and granted her more than the other seven young women, including her own attendants. When Esther was led to the king, she was very pleasing to him.

When nightfall came, she was led in, and in the early morning, she was dismissed. When the king considered all the virgins, Esther was shown to be the most beautiful. And she found his personal favor and compassion, and he placed the royal diadem upon her head. Then the king held a splendid wedding feast for Esther and canceled the debts of all the lands.

Esther (Alpha): Chapter 2 Notes

1 Septuagint manuscript 319: Gogaios (Γογλιος)

- Codex Vaticanus: Gai (ܓܐܝ)
- Aleppo Codex: Hgy (הגי)
- Leningrad Codex: Hegai (הֵגַי)
- Codex Monacensis (VL 130): Hegai

As the four names are related, the Latin Hegai is used in this translation, as it is the most common English rendering of the name, and is similar to the Hebrew pronunciation.

2 Septuagint manuscript 319: Ioudaeos (ιουδλιος).
Translation: Judahite (or Judean)

- Codex Vaticanus (in chapter 1): Ioudaeos (ΙΟΥΔΑΙΟC).
Translation: Judahite (or Judean)

- Aleppo Codex: Yhwdy (יהודי). Translation: Judahite (or Jew, Jewish)

- Leningrad Codex: Yehudi (יְהוּדִי). Translation: Judahite (or Jew, Jewish)

- Vetus Latina (chapter 3): Iudaeus. Translation: Judahite (or Judean, Jew)

All four source texts mention that he was one of the exiles in Babylon, who Nebuchadnezzar had taken from Jerusalem, however, the Vaticanus and Masoretic versions also specify that he was a Judahite in this sentence when they detail his family history.

Esther (Alpha): Chapter 2 Notes

This has to be something that was added later in Judean history, likely after the segregation of the Samaritans from the other Judahites by Ezra the scribe. As both the Vaticanus and Masoretic versions originate in Judea, either under Greek rule or later in the Hasmonean dynasty, this addition makes sense politically in the era.

It does however imply that the two copies that originated in the Seleucid Dynasty, the Alpha and Vetus Latina versions, originated in a land where that segregation was not relevant, such as the Seleucid provinces of Babylonia or Persis. As there is no evidence that Mordecai ever visited Judea, it is not possible to interpret this term as meaning Judean, and so the term Judahite is used.

Esther (Alpha): Chapter 3

After this, it happened that King Xerxes elevated Haman the son of Amyntas the Bryge, and praised him and placed him above all his friends, so that all would bow and lower themselves to the ground before him. However, although everyone would bow to him following the king's orders, Mordecai would not bow before him. When the servants of the king saw that Mordecai would not bow before Haman, the servants of the king asked Mordecai, "Why do you disobey the king, and don't bow before Haman?"

He answered them that he was a Judahite, and they informed Haman about him. Now when Haman heard, he was provoked to jealousy against Mordecai, and rage burned within him to the point he was seeking to destroy Mordecai and all his people on one day. Once Haman was provoked. and all his rage was stirred up, he turned red, and drove him from his sight. With maliciousness in his heart, he continuously spoke evil to the king regarding Israel, saying, "There are a people scattered throughout all the kingdoms, a people of war and rebellion, who have different laws from your laws, my king. They do not pay attention, though they are known among all nations because they are evil, and they ignore your commands to undermine your glory. Therefore, if it pleases the king and this judgment is good in his heart, let this nation be given to me for destruction, and I will pay into the treasury ten thousand talents of silver."

The king answered him, "Keep the silver, but do whatever you want to the nation." The king took his signet ring from his hand and gave it to Haman, adding, "Write to all the lands, and seal it with the signet ring of the king. For there is none who will reject the seal."

Haman went to his gods to learn the day of their death and cast lots for the thirteenth day of the month of Adar-Nisan[1] to murder all the Judahites, including men and women, and to take their young children as slaves. Then he rushed to give it into the hands of swift couriers.

This was the letter:

The great king Xerxes writes this to the rulers and lesser satraps of 127 districts from India to Kush. Ruling over many nations and the master of the whole world, I thought, not elated by the confidence of power, but ever conducting myself with great moderation and gentleness, to make the lives of my subjects continually tranquil, making my kingdom peaceful and open for travelers to its utmost limits, and to restore the peace desired by all people.

When I had inquired of my counselors how this might be accomplished. Haman, who excels in sound of judgment among us, and through unchanging goodwill and steadfast fidelity obtained the second place in the kingdom, informed us that there are scattered a certain ill-disposed people mixed among all the tribes throughout the world, who have laws in opposition to those of every nation and, on the other, continually disregard the command of kings so that the kingdom can never attain stability.

Therefore, as we understand that the nation stands alone in its way of life, which is contrary to all other people on account of an alienating way of life due to their laws, and since it is ill-disposed to our commands, it perpetually does the worst harm, so that we may never be established in the sole-rule directed by us, we order to you to destroy every one of those indicated to you in the letter written by Haman, who is set over the public affairs and is our second father. Include the women and children. May the daggers of their enemies, without pitying or restraint, on the fourteenth day of the twelfth month, this is Adar (which is Dystros),[2] eliminate the Judahites, and take their children as slaves, so the people who have long been hostile to us, and continue to be, are violently consigned to Hades[3] in one day.

May the time afterward be peaceful for us continually, and never again furnish us with matters for concern.

The decree was posted in Susa.

Esther (Alpha): Chapter 3 Notes

1 Septuagint manuscript 319: Adar Nisa (ᎠᎯᏓ ᏂᏍᎯ).

Translation: Adar-Nisan

- Codex Vaticanus: Adar (ᎠᎠᎯᏓ)
- Aleppo Codex: Ådr (אדר)
- Leningrad Codex: Adar (אֲדָר)
- Codex Monacensis (VL 130): Adar

The Alpha version is the only one of the four source texts that use the name Adar-Nisan, like in chapter 1, and again this year in Xerxes reign, 474 BC, was a leap year meaning there was a second month of Adar. Conversely, this year in Artaxerxes I's reign, 453 BC, was not a leap year, and so there was not a second month of Adar.

2 Septuagint manuscript 319: Adar (ᎠᎯᏓ)

- Codex Vaticanus: Adar (ᎠᎠᎯᏓ)
- Masoretic Text: the name is not included
- Codex Monacensis (VL 130): Adar

The Alpha version shows a difference between this reference to Adar, and the former reference to Adar-Nisan, implying that the letter that was being sent out throughout the empire was referring to the Adar twelve months after the Adar the letter was written in. This would make the month Adar, not Adar Bet, which seems to be what the Alpha version is recording. The Alpha version's translator also confirmed that Adar was Dystros (Δύστρος), the equivalent on the Macedonian calendar.

3 Septuagint manuscript 319: Hadên (ܐܝܕܠܢ). Translation: Hades (Greek god of the underworld), Hades (underworld), grave, death

• Codex Vaticanus: Aedên (ܐܝܕHN). Translation: Hades (Greek god of the underworld), Hades (underworld), grave, death

• Masoretic Text: the name is not included

• Codex Monacensis (VL 130): Orcus. Translation: Orcus (Roman god of the underworld), Orcus (underworld), grave, death

Esther (Alpha): Chapter 4

When Mordecai heard what was done, and the city of Susa was in chaos because of everything that had happened, as for all the Judahites there was great and terrible sorrow in the whole city. Mordecai went to his home, folded up his clothes, and put on sackcloth. After he had sprinkled ashes on himself, he went out as far as the outer courtyard and stood there, for he could not enter the royal palace in sackcloth. He called one of the eunuchs and sent him to Esther, and the queen stated, "Take off his sackcloth, and bring him in."

He did not want to, and instead, he replied, "Tell her this, 'Don't stop from going to the king and flattering him for the sake of me and my people. Remember your humble days when you were raised by my hand, because Haman, who is the second in command, has spoken to the king against us to put us to death. Therefore call upon God, and speak about us to the king, and deliver us from death!'"

Once he had informed her of the tribulation of Israel, she replied, "You know as well as anyone that whoever goes to the king uninvited, whomever he does not point out his golden scepter will be subject to death. I have not been called to him for thirty days. So how can I go now, not being invited?"

Mordecai replied to her, "If you ignore your nation and do not help them, then surely God will be a helper for them, and a deliverance, but you and your father's household will perish. Who knows if it was for this you were made queen?"

Then the queen sent a messenger saying, "Proclaim a religious service, and petition God earnestly, and I and my girls will do the same. I will go to the king uninvited, even if it is necessary that I die."

Mordecai did this, then he petitioned the Lord, remembering his works.

He said, "Lord Almighty,[1] under whose authority are all things and there is no one who can resist you when it is your will to save the house of Israel, because you have made the sky and land and every wonderful thing that is under the sky, and you rule everything. You know all things, and you know the race of Israel. It was not in insolence, nor for any love of glory that I did not bow down to this uncircumcised Haman, since I would have been willing to kiss the soles of his feet for the sake of Israel, but I did this so that I might not set anyone above your glory, Lord, and not bow to anyone but you, the trustworthy, and I will not do it even under duress. Now, Lord, you who covenanted with Abraham, spare your people, because they plan to ruin us, and they desire to take away the inheritance that has been yours from the beginning. Do not neglect your portion, which you redeemed out of the land of Egypt. Listen to our petition, and have mercy upon your inheritance. Turn our mourning into rejoicing, that we may live and sing hymns to you. Do not silence the mouth of those who sing hymns to you."

Queen Esther searched for herself a refuge in the Lord, being taken as it were in the agony of death. Having taken off her glorious apparel, and every sign of her splendor, and she put on garments of distress and mourning instead of expensive perfumes, she filled her head with ashes and dung, and she greatly humbled her body, every sign of her beauty and adornment she covered humbly with her lovely hair.

She implored the Lord, "Lord Moloch,[2] you alone are a helper, help me. I am humble and have no helper except you, for my danger is near at hand. I have heard from the book of my tribe that you, took Israel out of all the nations, and our fathers out of all their families, and appointing Israel over them for an eternal inheritance. You worked for them all that you have said. We have sinned before you, and you have delivered us into the hands of our enemies because we honored their gods."

"You are righteous, Lord, but now they have not been contented with the bitterness of our slavery, but have laid their hands on the hands of their idols, in order to abolish the decree of your mouth, and completely destroy your inheritance, and to stop the mouth of those who praise you and to extinguish the glory of your temple and your altar, and to open the mouth of the enemies for the mighty deeds of vain. Lord, do not resign your scepter to enemies who hate you, and don't let them laugh at our fall, but turn their counsel against them, and make a public example of him who begun to injure us. Remember us, Lord, manifest yourself in the time of our affliction, and do not break us. Put harmonious speech into my mouth, and give favor to my words, and turn his heart to hate he who fights against us, to the utter destruction of those that consent with him. But deliver us by your strong hand, and help me as you know everything, and you know that I abhor the bed of the uncircumcised, and hate the glory of the lawless and of any alien."

"You, Lord, know my necessity, for I abhor the symbol of my proud station, which is on my head in the days of my splendor. I abhor it like the cloth of a woman that sits apart. Your servant has not eaten with them at their table, and I have not honored the banquet of the king, nor have I drunk wine of libations. Your slave has not rejoiced since the day of my promotion until now, except in you, Lord. You who has power over all things, listen to the voice of the desperate, and deliver us from the hand of those who evil against us, and take me, Lord, out of the grip of my fear!"

Esther (Alpha): Chapter 4 Notes

1 Septuagint manuscript 319: Cyrie pantocratôr (Κ ब̄ρıϭ πλντοιβαν̄τοοβ). Translation: Lord Omnipotent (or Almighty)

- Codex Vaticanus: Cyrie Cyrie Basileu (ΚΥρıεΚΥρıε ΒΑϭıλεΥ). Translation: Lord Lord King

- Masoretic text: section missing

- Codex Monacensis (VL 130): deum Abraham, et deum Isaac, et deum Iacob. Translation: god of Abraham and god of Isaac and the god of Jacob

The three source texts with names, use terms that cannot be derived from each other, while the Masoretic version omits any name. This is an indicator of which Israelite group originally translated each version. It is unclear where the Masoretic version originated.

The Vetus Latina's version was likely translated by non-Judahite Israelites, somewhere in the Seleucid Empire, possibly in Damascus, where there had been a large Aramaic Israelite community since the era when Samaria ruled Aram. The references to Abraham, Isaac, and Jacob were more commonly found among the Israelites that Ezra rejected circa 351 BC, many of which later resettled in southern Egypt during the wars between the Seleucids and Ptolemys between 300 and 200 BC. These Israelites were mostly driven out of Egypt in 200 BC, when the province of Judea rebelled against the rule of Ptolemy's Egypt. This means the original Greek translation of the Vetus Latina version, was likely made in the 3rd century BC. The Testaments of Abraham, Isaac, and Jacob continued to be used by the Beta

Israel and Beta Abraham communities in Sudan and Ethiopia, however, the version of Esther adopted by the Ethiopian Tewahedo Church was the Vaticanus version, which is believed to have been translated from the Greek.

While the Vetus Latina version, or one like it, was used in Egypt, it is unclear if the Beta Abraham community continues to use a version of Esther. The two Greek versions are more consistent with the Septuagint, as both Lord and Lord Almighty are both used in various books of the Septuagint. The later use of the term Lord God King in the Vaticanus version, and Lord King, in the Vetus Latina both point to the original god in the text being Moloch, which explains why the Masoretic version was stripped of any reference to any god, and why random substitutions appear to have happened in the other versions.

In this case, the Alpha's Lord Almighty is translated directly, although the rest of the paragraph does make it clear that the god in the original text was regarded as a king.

2 Septuagint manuscript 319: Cyrie basileus (Κ ᾱϼιϭ βᾱσιλϭὺς). Translation: Lord King

• Codex Vaticanus: Cyrie mou o basileus (ΚΥΡΙΕΜΟΥΟ ΒΑϹΙΛΕΥϹ). Translation: my Lord the King

• Masoretic text: section missing

• Codex Monacensis (VL 130): deum Abraham, et deum Isaac, et deum Iacob. Translation: God of Abraham and God of Isaac and the God of Jacob

While the Alpha and Vaticanus version of the term could be derived from a common source, the Vetus Latina's phrase is clearly a substitution. All three of the source texts other than the Masoretic texts, do at some point used the phrase Lord King (Κύριε Βασιλεὺς or Dominus Rex), as well as the Vaticanus' version's Lord God King (Κύριε ο θεὸς ο βασιλεὺς).

The Alpha Texts' Lord King is curious, as it can only be translated back into Aramaic as Lord Melech (ᵓᔕ᷄ᴎᵓᴎᵓ). The various translations of the Lord King in the Codex Vaticanus and Vetus Latina seem to confirm the Aramaic source text used the term. The usage of the name King: mlkå (ᴎᴊᐸᔕ) for the god in question renders as the name Moloch, which is a proper name of a god, that happened to be spelled the same way as the word king in Aramaic: mlkå (ᴎᴊᐸᔕ), Hebrew: mlk (מֶלֶךְ), Canaanite: mlk (𐤌𐤋𐤊), and Syriac: mlkå (ܡܠܟܐ).

That the Judahites were worshiping a god named Moloch is not debated, King Josiah banned Moloch's worship in 625 BC, when he promoted Yhwh to be the Judahite national god, however, based on the writings of Baruch, it is clear that the Judahites reverted to the old gods after Josiah died. These references to Moloch do make sense in relation to Mordecai's name as Marduk was the king of the Babylonian gods, and so Mordecai was named after the Babylonian version of Moloch. This also explains why the Masoretic version had all references to God stripped from it, as the book was about a prophet of the wrong god.

The additions of the set of names 'Abraham, Isaac, and Jacob,' found in the Vetus Latina version also makes sense, as the translators seem to have been trying to justify Moloch by stating he was the god of the three ancient patriarchs. The Judahites and Israelites in southern Egypt never stopped using the name Moloch, and carried it south with them into Sudan and Ethiopia, and the Ge'ez (and Amharic) word for 'God' continues to be Ämlak (አምላክ) to this day, derived from the ancient Semitic word for king. As the original meaning of the name translated as King was clearly Moloch, that name is restored.

Esther (Alpha): Chapter 5

On the third day when Esther had ceased praying, she took off her humble dress and put on her glorious apparel. Being splendidly clothed, and having called on the all-knowing preserver God, she took her two servers, and she leaned on one gently for support, and the other followed carrying her train. She was blooming in the perfection of her beauty, and her face was cheerful, but her heart was in anguish.

Having passed through all the doors, she stood before the king. The king was sitting on his throne of his kingdom, clothed in all his glorious apparel, covered all over with gold and precious stones. He was very terrible. Having raised his face resplendent with glory, he looked right at her like a bull in intense anger. The queen was terrified and her face turned pale from faintness, and she leaned on the head of the girl who went before her.

But God changed the spirit of the king and turned his anger to gentleness, and alarmed, the king sprang down from his throne and took her into his arms. He comforted her, saying, "What is the matter, Esther? I am your brother. Take heart, you will not die, for our command is only for the common person. The threat is not against you. Know the scepter is in your hand."

Having raised the golden scepter he laid it on her neck. He embraced her, and said, "Speak to me."

She said to him, "I saw you like a messenger god,[1] and my heart melted from the glory of your rage, Lord."

Her face was sweating, and the king and his servants were troubled, and they comforted her. The king asked, "What do you want, Esther? Tell me, and I will do it for you, up to half of my kingdom."

Esther replied, "Tomorrow is a great day for me. If then it seems good to the king, then could you and Haman, your friend, come to a wine feast which I will prepare tomorrow?"

The king ordered, "Bring Haman quickly, that we may do as Esther requests."

They both went to the feast which Esther had made, a veritable banquet, and the king asked Esther, "My queen, what is your request? Ask up to half my kingdom, and it shall be yours, whatever you ask."

Esther answered, "This is my petition and my request, if I have found favor before you, king, and if it pleases the king to grant my petition and to do my request, let the king and Haman come to the dinner that I will prepare for them again tomorrow. For again tomorrow I will do likewise."

So the king said, "Do as you want."

It was heard by Haman and he marveled, and the king departed and retired. Haman went into his home, and gathered together his friends, his sons and Zosaran[2] his wife. He boasted saying, "The queen has called no one to the feast with the king but me, and I am invited tomorrow. But this thing did not please me, while I was there, I saw Mordecai the Judahite in the court of the king. He does not bow down to me."

Then Zosaran his wife said to him, "He is from the race of the Judahites. Since the king has allowed you to destroy the Judahites and the gods have given you a day of destruction to take revenge on them, let a pole fifty cubits high be cut for you, and be set up, and hang him on the pole. Early in the morning you can speak to the king about him, but now go, and celebrate with the king."

The idea pleased Haman, and so he did it.

Esther (Alpha): Chapter 5 Notes

1 Septuagint manuscript 319: angelon theou (ἀγγόλον θόου). Translation: messenger god

• Codex Vaticanus: angelon theou (ⲀⲄⲄⲈⲗⲞⲚⲐⲈⲞⲨ). Translation: messenger god

• Masoretic Text: section missing

• Codex Monacensis (VL 130): angelus dei. Translation: messenger god

2 Septuagint manuscript 319: Zôsaran (Ζωσαϸὰν)

• Codex Vaticanus: Zôsaran (ΖⲱⲥⲀⲢⲀⲚ)

• Aleppo Codex: Zrš (זרש)

• Leningrad Codex: Zeresh (זֶ֫רֶשׁ)

• Codex Monacensis (VL 130): Zosarra

As the names all appear to derive from a common name, however, the Aramaic text is lost, the Greek name is used in this translation.

Esther (Alpha): Chapter 6

The Lord would not allow the king to sleep that night, and he stayed awake. The readers were called, and the court record was read to him.

There was the record of the eunuchs and what good deed Mordecai had done for the king. The king thought seriously on that matter, and said, "Mordecai is a loyal man for protecting my life, for he has kept me alive even until now, and I am sitting on my throne today and have done nothing for him. I have not done right by him."

The king asked his servants, "What should we do for Mordecai, my savior in these matters?"

They thought about it, but the young men were envious of him, as fear of Haman lay in their bowels, and the king understood.

In the morning, the king asked, "Who is outside?" It was Haman.

Haman had come early to speak to the king so that he could hang Mordecai, and the king ordered to bring him in. As he entered, the king asked him, "What should we do for the man who honors the king? For one who the king wishes to honor?"

Haman thought, 'Who would the king honor other than me?' and so Haman answered, "As for the man who the king wishes to honor, let a royal robe be brought, and a royal horse on which the king rides, and let one of the king's noblest friends take these things and clothe him, and let him mount him on the horse, and go around the city before him proclaiming. This should be done for the one who honors the king, and who the king wishes to honor."

The king said to Haman, "Run quickly, and take the horse and robe as you have said, and do so to Mordecai the Judahite who sits at the gateway. Don't let your word be neglected."

So Haman took the robe and the horse, and clothed Mordecai, and mounted him on the horse, and went through the streets of the city, and proclaimed, "This will be for every man who the king wishes to honor."

When Haman realized that it was not he who would be honored, but that it was Mordecai, his heart was utterly broken, and his spirit became feeble. Haman took the robe and the horse, showing reverence to Mordecai on the exact same day that he'd intended to impale him. He said to Mordecai, "Take off the sackcloth."

Mordecai was distressed like one dying, and with anguish he took off the sackcloth and put on the glorious clothes. Mordecai thought he saw a sign, and his heart was toward the Lord, and he was mystified in silent fear.

Haman rushed to put him on horseback, and Haman led the horse outside and walked before him proclaiming, "This will be done for the man who honors the king, who the king wishes to honor."

Haman returned to his home downhearted, and Mordecai went to his home. Haman told his wife everything that had happened to him. His wife and his wise men said, "Ever since you spoke evil about him, evil things have been coming to you. Be quiet, because God is among them."

While they were still speaking, someone arrived to rush him alone to the wine festival, and so he was cheered up, and when he had traveled the distance, he reclined with them at the appointed time.

Esther (Alpha): Chapter 7

As the drinking advanced, the king asked Esther, "What is the danger, and what is your petition? Ask up to half of my kingdom!"

Esther struggled with her reply, because the enemy was before her eyes, and God gave her courage as she called upon him. Esther answered, "If it pleases the king and the decision is good in his heart, let my people be given for my petition, and my nation for my life. For I and my people have been sold into slavery and the young children as plunder. I did not want to tell you, in case I trouble my lord, as the man who did evil against us has changed his manner."

The king became angry and demanded, "Who is this that has dared to humiliate the sign of my rule so as to disregard the fear of you?"

When the queen saw that it seemed a grave offense to the king and that he hated evil, she said, "Do not be angry, lord, for it is enough that I have found your conciliation. Enjoy your meal, king, and tomorrow I will do according to your word."

The king swore that she must tell him who was so arrogant to do this, and with an oath he took it upon himself to do for her whatever she wished. So Esther was brave and answered, "Haman, your friend, is this liar, this evil man!"

The king became angry and filled with rage, and jumped up and left to walk around. Haman was terrified and bowed himself at the feet of Queen Esther as she still reclined on her couch. Just then the king returned to the banquet, and when he saw this he said, "A crime against my kingdom is not enough for you? Would you also rape my wife in my presence? Let Haman be taken away, and don't let him live!" And so he was taken away.

Then Agathas,[1] one of his servants, said, "Know that there is a pole in his courtyard fifty cubits tall, which Haman cut down to hang Mordecai, the man who spoke good things concerning the king, therefore, lord, order that he himself be hanged upon it."

The king ordered, "Let him be hanged on it," and the king removed the signet ring from his hand, and his life was sealed with it.

The king said to Esther, "He even planned to hang Mordecai, who saved me from the hand of the eunuchs? Didn't he know that Esther is of his race?"

The king called Mordecai and granted him all that belonged to Haman, and he asked him, "What do you want? I will do it for you."

Mordecai answered, "That you revoke Haman's letter." Then the king entrusted him with the affairs of the kingdom.

Then Esther said to the king on the next day, "Allow me to punish my enemies with bloodshed."

Queen Esther appealed to the king also against Haman's children, that they too should die with their father. And the king said, "Let it be done," so she struck the enemies in great numbers. In Susa, the king made an agreement with the queen to kill men, and he said, "Know that I give them to you to hang," and it was done.

He wrote the following letter:

The great king Xerxes to the rulers of the 127 lands from India to Kush and to the satraps who are faithful to our interests, greetings.

Many people who have been frequently honored with the greatest kindness of their benefactors have become more ambitious, not only seek to harm those subject to us, but not being able to deal with prosperity, they even undertake to scheme evil against their own benefactors.

They not only take away gratitude from among people, but have gone astray due to the bragging of those who are inexperienced in goodness, they even imagine they will escape the evil-hating justice of the Just Judge[2] who rules all things.

Oftentimes after having been appointed to places of authority to administer the affairs of trusting friends, has caused them to be partakers of the shedding of innocent blood, and they brought about irremediable calamities, beguiling with the lies and deceit they misconstrue the sincere goodwill of their sovereigns.

It is possible to see from the records that have been handed down to us, and to the extent that we duly see what lies at our feet due to the savagery of those that hold power, to pay attention with regard to the future, that we may maintain the government in undisturbed peace, since we do not utilize slanders but manage the matters that come to our attention with consideration.

For while Haman the son of Amyntas the Bryge,[3] who was in truth an alien to the thinking of the Persians and quite devoid from kindness, having obtained so fully the goodwill from us for every nation to such an extent that he was publicly proclaimed our father, and was continually done obeisance to by all as the second person to the royal thrones. But, unable to restrain his arrogance, he undertook to divest us of our rule and our breath and by crafty ruses finagled to destroy Mordecai, our constant savior, and Esther, his innocent partner, together with their whole nation. For when by these methods he had caught us undefended, he thought that he would bring about an alienation of the rule of the Persians to the Macedonians.[4] But we find that the Judahites, who have been consigned to you by this triple-cursed man, are not criminals, but governed by the most just laws, and are the sons of the only and true God,[5] who gave our ancestors the kingdom and maintains it in good order.

Therefore, do not pay attention to the letter sent by Haman, because he who has done these things, has been impaled at the gates of Susa, since the Judge who sees all things has repaid him with the deserved penalty. Let this letter be published in every place, so the Judahites may live by their own laws, and to help them, so they might defend themselves against those who attack them at the time of oppression. It has been decided by the Judahites through-out the kingdom to observe the fourteenth day of the month, which is Adar, and to hold a feast on the fifteenth, because on those days the Omnipotent[6] has made for them deliverance and rejoicing.

From now on they rightly mean deliverance for the Per-sians and a memorial of destruction for those who plotted against them. Every city and land that does not do this, by spear and fire shall be consumed in wrath. It shall be stretched out not only impassable for people but also for wild animals and birds.

A public ordinance containing these things was published in Susa, and the king authorized Mordecai to write whatever he wanted. Mordecai sent out letters and sealed them with the king's signet ring, saying that his people should each remain in their own land and celebrate a feast to God. The letter which Mordecai sent said this:

> Haman sent to you letters stating, "Rush quickly to send the disobedient nation of the Judahites to me for destruction.' But I, Mordecai, inform you that the one who did this has been hung at the gates of Susa, and his family has been killed, as this one wanted to kill us on the thirteenth of the month of Adar.'"

Then Mordecai went out wearing the royal clothing and a diadem of purple linen, and when the people in Susa saw him they rejoiced. For the Judahites, there was light, drinking, and feasting. Many of the Judahites were circumcised, and no one rose up against them as they feared them.

The chiefs and the rulers of the satraps and the royal scribes, honored the Judahites, for the fear of Mordecai was on them. In Susa, Haman was referred to by name, and so were the enemies throughout the whole kingdom. In Susa, the Judahites murdered seven hundred men,[7] including Pharsan and his brother and Pharna, and Gagaphardatha, Marmasaima, and Izathouth,[8] and the ten sons of Haman the son of Amyntas the Bryge, the enemy of the Judahites, and they plundered all their property.

He asked Esther, "How have your people here and in the surrounding lands fared?"

Esther answered the king, "Let it be granted to the Judahites to murder and plunder whomever they want." He agreed, and they killed 70,100 men."

Mordecai recorded these things in a book and sent it to the Judahites who were in the kingdom of Xerxes, both far and near, to keep these days for hymns and rejoicing in the place of pain and grief, the fourteenth and fifteenth. He also sent portions to the poor, and they welcomed them. Because of this these days are called Purim,[9] because of the lots that fell on these days as a memorial.

The king recorded the tax of land and sea, and strength, both the riches and the glory of his kingdom. Mordecai praised him and wrote in the books of the Persians and Medes as a memorial. Mordecai was viceroy to King Xerxes, and was a great man in the kingdom, and honored by the Judahites, and passed his life beloved of all his nation.

Mordecai said, "These things have come from God. For I remember the dream which I had."

It was fulfilled, and he said, "The little fountain is Esther. The two dragons are myself and Haman. The river are those nations that combined to destroy the Judahites. The sun and light are the revelation of God that appeared to the Judahites. This is the judgment. God has worked these signs and wonders, as have not been done among the nations. Then he ordained two lots. One for the people of God, and one for all the other nations. These two lots approached the hours at the right time and day of the lordship of the everlasting one among all the nations. God remembered his people and vindicated his inheritance. All the people cried out in a loud voice and said, "Blessed are you, Lord, who remembers the covenants made with our fathers, Amen!"

These days in the month Adar, on the fourteenth and the fifteenth day of the month, will be observed by them with a gathering and joy and gladness before God, from generation to generation for ever among his people Israel.

Esther (Alpha): Chapter 7 Notes

1 Septuagint manuscript 319: Agathas (ϕγᴁθᴁc)

- Codex Vaticanus: Bougathan (ʙoϒᴦᴀѳᴀɴ)

- Aleppo Codex: Ḥrbwnh (חרבונה)

- Leningrad Codex: Charvovnah (חַרְבֹונָֿה)

- Codex Monacensis (VL 130): Buzatas

As none of the source texts agree on the name, the Alpha version's name is transliterated.

2 Septuagint manuscript 319: molis critês (μꙅλιc ꙙ𝑃ιτρc). Translation: just judge

- Codex Vaticanus: epicratountos theou (ᴇᴨικ𝑃ᴀᴛoϒɴᴛocѳᴇoϒ) Translation: prevailing god

- Masoretic Text: the letter is missing from the chapter

- Codex Monacensis (VL 130): Deus qui scrutatur. Translation: god who examines

3 Septuagint manuscript 319: Bougaeos (ϐoυγᴁιoc)

- Codex Vaticanus: Macedôn (ᴍᴀκᴇᴅꙍɴ). Translation: Macedonian

- Masoretic Text: the letter is missing from the chapter

- Codex Monacensis (VL 130): Macedonica

This reference to Haman, confirms that the translators of the Vaticanus and Vetus Latina versions considered the term found in the Aramaic source texts to mean 'Macedonian,' as the translator of the Alpha version translated the term earlier, where the Masoretic texts use the term Agagai (אֲגָגִי). Unlike the earlier reference to Haman in the Vaticanus version, where he was praised, in this case, he is being denounced by the king, and therefore it would have not been objectionable to Ptolemy V and seems to have been left in the text.

The meaning of the word Bougaeos (Βουγαιος) in Alpha version, as well as in chapter 1 of the Vaticanus version where it is used in the same way it is here in the Alpha version, is an unknown term, however, sometimes translated as bully or braggart. As it is used as a substitute for Macedonian in both places, it is likely an attempt to transliterate Brygoe (Βρύγοι) back into Greek from Aramaic. The Brygoe, more commonly called the Bryges in English, were a tribe of people that settled in Macedonia, northern Greece, and Albania shortly before the Persians invaded Greece.

4 Septuagint manuscript 319: Macedôn (Ⲙⲁⲗⲅⲁⲇⲱⲛ).

Translation: Macedonian

• Codex Vaticanus: Macedôn (Ⲙⲁⲕⲉⲇⲱⲛ). Translation: Macedonian

• Masoretic Text: the letter is missing from the chapter

• Codex Monacensis (VL 130): Macedonica

All of the versions of the letter specifically refer to the Macedonians, and accuse Haman of plotting with them in an attempt to overthrow the Persian government.

5 Septuagint manuscript 319: mono cae alêthinos Theos (μƍνο 界Δι ἀλ界θιɴƍc Θ6ƍc). Translation: only and true God

• Codex Vaticanus: hypsistou megistou zôntos Theou (ΥϯιϲΤΟΥ ΜεΓιϲΤΟΥ ΖѠΝΤΟϹ ϴΕΟΥ). Translation: highest supreme living god

• Masoretic Text: the letter is missing from the chapter

• Codex Monacensis (VL 130): excelsis deo. Translation: highest God

The Vaticanus and Vetus Latina versions of Esther both refer to the 'highest God,' suggesting that this was in the Aramaic text that was translated. As Xerxes I was a Zoroastrian, this likely started out as the Zoroastrian title of Ahura Mazda: A-frajdum (افراجـدم) meaning 'Highest.' The full title in the Vaticanus version appears to be the Zoroastrian title A-frajdum Aekh Tan (افراجـدم ائيـک تن) meaning 'Highest Supreme Soul,' which, if the translators still recognized it when the Alpha and Vetus Latina translations were made, would explain their redactions of the name. In any event, if the letter was published in the name of Xerxes, the god being referenced was Ahura Mazda.

As the three source texts do not agree on the titles of the god, the titles are translated directly from the Alpha Text version in this translation.

6 Septuagint manuscript 319: pantocratôr (παντοκρατωρ). Translation: omnipotent (or almighty)

- Codex Vaticanus: theou (ΘΕΟΥ). Translation: god
- Masoretic Text: section missing
- Codex Monacensis (VL 130): term missing

7 Septuagint manuscript 319: andras ephtacosia (ανδρας εφτακοσια). Translation: seven hundred men

- Codex Vaticanus: andras pentacosious (ΑΝΔΡΑC ΠΕΝΤΑΚΟCΙΟΥC). Translation: five hundred men
- Aleppo Codex: ḥmš måwt {R} åyš {S} (חמש מאות {ר} איש {ס}) Translation: five hundred (R) men (S)
- Leningrad Codex: chamesh me'ovt ish (חֲמֵשׁ מֵאוֹת אִישׁ). Translation: five hundred men
- Codex Monacensis (VL 130): this section is missing

8 Septuagint manuscript 319: Pharsan cae o aderphos tou cae ê Pharna cae ê Gagaphardatha cae ê Marmasaema cae Izathouth (Φαρσαν και ο αδερφος του και η Φαρνα και η

ΓΑγΑ$ΑΡΑΑΘΑ ιιΑι ῾Ι ΜΑΡμΑσΑιμΑ ιιΑι ιΖΑθουθ). Translation: Pharsan and his brother and Pharna and Gagaphardatha and Marmasaima and Izathouth

- Codex Vaticanus: Pharsannestaen cae Delphôn cae Phasga cae Phardatha cae Barea cae Sarbacha cae Marmasima cae Arouphaeon cae Arsaeon cae Zabouthaethan (ΦΑΡCΑΝΝΕCΤΑΙΝ ΚΑΙ ΔΕΛΦωΝ ΚΑΙ ΦΑCΓΑ ΚΑΙ ΦΑΡΔΑΘΑΚΑΙΒΑΡΕΑΚΑΙCΑΡΒΑΧΑΚΑΙΜΑΡΜΑCΙΜΑΚΑΙ ΑΡΟΥΦΑΙΟΝ ΚΑΙ ΑΡCΑΙΟΝ ΚΑΙ ΖΑΒΟΥΘΑΙΘΑΝ). Translation: Pharsannestaen and Delphôn and Phasga and Phardatha and Barea and Sarbacha and Marmasima and Arouphaeon and Arsaeon and Zabouthaethan

- Aleppo Codex: pršndtå [s] wåt [r] dlpwn [s] wåt [r] åsptå [s] 8 wåt [r] pwrtå [s] wåt [r] ådlyå [s] wåt [r] årydtå [s] 9 wåt [r] prmštå [s] wåt [r] årysy [s] wåt [r] årydy [s] wåt [r] wyztå [s] (פרשנדתא [ס] ואת [ר] דלפון [ס] ואת [ר] אספתא [ס] ח ואת [ר] פורתא) [ס] ואת [ר] אדליא [ס] ואת [ר] ארידתא [ס] ט ואת [ר] פרמשתא [ס] ואת [ר] אריסי [ס] ואת [ר] ארידי [ס] ואת [ר] ויזתא [ס]). Translation: Pršndtå [S] and [R] Dlpwn [S] and [R] Åsptå [S] 8 and [R] Pwrtå [S] and [R] Ådlyå [S] and [R] Årydtå [S] and [R] Prmštå [S] and [R] Årysy [S] and [R] Årydy [S] and [R] Wyztå [S]

- Leningrad Codex: parshandata ve'et - dalfovn ve'et - aspata ve'et - povrata ve'et - adalya ve'et - aridata ve'et - parmashta ve'et - arisai ve'et - aridai ve'et – vayzata (פַּרְשַׁנְדָּתָא וְאֵת – דַּלְפוֹן וְאֵת – אַסְפָּתָא וְאֵת – פּוֹרָתָא וְאֵת –) אֲדַלְיָא וְאֵת – אֲרִידָתָא וְאֵת – פַּרְמַשְׁתָּא וְאֵת – אֲרִיסַי וְאֵת – אֲרִדַי וְאֵת (אֵת – וַיְזָתָא). Translation: Parshandata and Dalfovn and Aspata

195

and Povrata and Adalya and Aridata and Parmashta and Arisai
and Aridai and Vayzata

• Codex Monacensis (VL 130): this section is missing

Both the Vaticanus and Masoretic versions name ten people,
which are implied to be the ten sons of Haman, while the
Alpha version names five people, and then states the ten sons
of Haman were also killed.

9 Septuagint manuscript 319: Phrourae (Ⲫⲃⲟⲩⲣⲁⲓ).
Translation: Purim

• Codex Vaticanus: Phrourae (Ⲫⲣⲟⲩⲣⲁⲓ). Translation:
Purim

• Aleppo Codex: pwrym (פורים)

• Leningrad Codex: pûrîm (פּוּרִים)

• Codex Monacensis (VL 130): epistula custodientium.
Translation: letter guardians

The Latin is believed to be a mistranslation of the Greek tôn
Phrourae (των Φρουραι).

Septuagint Manuscripts

The following is a list of the Septuagint manuscripts referenced in the notes for this book.

LXX B (Codex Vaticanus) is dated to the 4th century. It is currently located at the Vatican Library (Gr. 1209) in Vatican City.

LXX 19 is dated to the 12th century. It is currently located at the Chigi Palace (R. VI. 38) in Rome.

LXX 93 is dated to the 13th century. It is currently located at the British Library (Royal 1 D. II) in London.

LXX 108 is dated the 13th century. It is currently located at the Vatican Library (Gr. 330) in Vatican City.

LXX 319 is dated to 1021. It is currently located at the Vatopedi monastery (600) on Mount Athos.

LXX 996 (Oxyrhynchus Papyrus LXV 4443) is dated to 1st century. It is currently located in the Ashmolean Museum (LXV 4443), in Oxford.

Alternative Translations

The following is a list of alternative translations that were used for comparative analysis.

The Aleppo Codex is dated to circa 920 AD. For centuries it was housed at the Central Synagogue of Aleppo, from which its name is derived. It was the oldest known complete copy of the Hebrew scriptures used within Judaism until 1947, when it was seized and divided among Jewish families during anti-Jewish riots in Aleppo. The sections that have resurfaced are currently at the Israel Museum in Jerusalem. Approximately 40% is still missing.

The Leningrad Codex is dated to 1008 (or 1009) AD. It is currently located at the National Library of Russia (Firkovich B 19 A) in St. Petersburg. The Leningrad Codex is the oldest complete copy of the Hebrew scriptures used within Judaism.

The Vetus Latina are the old Latin translations of the Septuagint and other Israelite texts that predate Jerome's Latin Orthodox Bible in the 5th century. Some of the texts appear to have been translated directly from Aramaic or Hebrew source texts, however, most appear to have been translations from the Greek translations. The version of Esther found in the Vetus Latina manuscripts is far closer to the Alpha Texts version of Esther than the more common versions found in the majority of Septuagint manuscripts, suggesting it was translated from an Aramaic source.

The Codex Monacensis (VL 130) is a copy of the books of Tobit, Judith, and Esther which dates to 800. It is currently located at the Bavarian State Library (Clm 6239), in Munich.

Also Available

ALSO AVAILABLE

- Octateuch: The Original Orit

ENOCH AND METATRON SERIES:
- Books of Enoch Collection

- Books of Enoch and Metatron Collection

- Books of Metatron Collection

- Secrets of Enoch

OTHER TRANSLATIONS:
- Apocalypses of Ezra

- Arabic Maccabees

- Life of Adam and Eve

- Memories of the New Kingdom

- Septuagint's Esther and the Vetus Latina Esther

- Septuagint's Ezekiel and the Ba'al Cycle

- Septuagint's Job and the Testament of Job

- Septuagint's Proverbs and the Wisdom of Amenemope

- The Amarna Letters

- Testaments of the Patriarchs Collection

- Tobit and Ahikar

- Ugaritic Texts: Ba'al Cycle

- Wisdom of Ahikar

www.ingramcontent.com/pod-product-compliance
Lightning Source LLC
Chambersburg PA
CBHW061153120626
46546CB00005B/2039